FROM
BROKEN
TO
Beautiful

Lisa A. Hardwick

You are Worthy! Honor You! Love and Blessings! Lisa Hardwick

"Since winning NBC's The Biggest Loser, I have had the opportunity to travel the country and meet amazing people. Lisa Hardwick is one of those people. She has shown that regardless of circumstance, we are all capable of living extraordinary lives. Her story and message have reinforced the fact that before you can make a change in your life, you must make a change in your mind!"

~ Matt Hoover
Winner of NBC's Hit Reality Show The Biggest Loser

"What would it be like to pick up a book, and after reading just a few pages, have a voice in your head - your own voice - lovingly and gratefully say 'You're on your way home!'? From Broken to Beautiful is that book. When you first meet Lisa Hardwick, it's easy to conclude that you are with someone who has always had high self-esteem, and had her life on the fast track to success since her teenage years-or before; you feel that way, because of the way she makes YOU feel when she in nearby, but it hasn't been that long ago, that you would have met a very different Lisa. From Broken to Beautiful is a book of hope, love, peace, strength and Lisa opens your heart to new possibilities, by opening her heart to you. You'll be touched, and transformed forever!"

~ Vincent Harris
Body Language Expert and Author

"Lisa Hardwick is a warm, personable speaker and writer who shares an amazing insight into her personal life. Her courageous story of triumph in her life shows us that healing your life is indeed possible. Her genuine heart and spirit envelopes you and makes you feel safe with sharing your truths."

~ Shelly York
Owner of "Affirmations Rock"

"Lisa Hardwick is a creative talented writer. Her enthusiasm for life and all it has to offer is contagious to those she comes into contact with. The first thing I noticed about her was a pure spirit shining through her eyes. They draw you in with a warmth that shines from the depth of her soul. This flame is what she wishes to see in all. She has an uncanny ability to see the smoldering embers in those she meets. With a desire to see people obtain the tools to become what they were created to be she fans that ember with great care until there is a great bonfire that cannot be easily doused. Holding nothing back she shares her life story in the tradition of old. Hoping her story is passed on to all so that they might also find the courage to share their story. The stories of hope and healing."

~ Lisa Donahue
aka "Chicago Mermaid", Artist and Author of "7 Jars of Peanut Butter"

"Driven, visionary, make it happen despite the odds. A business woman full of grit and grace. Just a few of the ways I'd describe the dynamo that is Lisa Hardwick. If you want to make things happen and change your life forever then you've found the right woman at the right time. -But hang on... it's gonna be a wild ride!"

~ Dave Lakhani
Author of "Persuasion: The Art of Getting What You Want"

"From Broken to Beautiful would not have happened, were it not for one very shining star—Miss Lady Lisa—Lisa A Hardwick. Lisa is a powerful people magnet with a special talent for gathering those of like minds together. Once you meet Lisa, you realize you've met someone very special. It is because of Lisa's passion for truth, for God, for helping others find their own path from broken to beautiful that this book exists. Lisa touches lives for the better in her every thought, word and deed. Each day I am a better person, a more beautiful person for knowing Lisa. It is an honor and a true privilege to count her as a soul friend, to share her shining light."

~ Michelle Matteson
The Maven of the Mind

"The most successful and happiest people are those who know how to bring each situation into balance by reducing that which is too great, and adding to that which is too little. Such a person craves not power, but balanced and stable relationships. Regardless of her position, Lisa Hardwick has done, and continues to do just that. Through her own experiences, trials and errors, she has created a REAL approach to life's challenges. In Lisa's book, 'From Broken to Beautiful,' she breaks down the ugliness we believe as truth and replenishes us with authentic confidence in ourselves. No matter the hurdle any one of us is facing, there are workable solutions, and Lisa A. Hardwick is living proof!"

~ Heather Swango,
Excel Business Manager

"In her new book, 'From Broken to Beautiful,' Lisa spreads her gift of bringing out the best in others. By sharing her personal story of survival and teaching the tools that she used to provide instant relief, train her mind, and transform herself into a secure, confident, inspiring woman, Lisa reaches out to those who have never given themselves a chance to be their best. Lisa is a talented writer who not only talks the talk but also "walks the walk", and she is dedicated to helping those that are silently suffering from abuse so they may transform themselves from broken victims to beautiful survivors."

~ Kenneth L. Peplow
M.S. Illinois State University and Author

"Lisa Hardwick is extremely positive, hardworking, dependable and impressive with her down to earth charm. Lisa is not afraid to roll her sleeves up and dive right into the trenches with you to get the work done. She has much to share with her personal experiences and those around her get lifted."

~ David Youhas
Certified Performance Coach

"Lisa Hardwick has the compassion of Mother Teresa, the aggressiveness of a starved pit bull terrier yet effortlessly brews this concoction to delight the spirit of all who are privileged to be called her friend. To be her acquaintance, you have entered a society that requires deeper thought, with the overall strategy to make this a better world in which to live. Enjoy her, embrace her and you too shall shine. This girl has pizzazz!"

~ Jim Dye
Sales Executive

"One day, one moment, one conversation with Lisa will and can change your direction, perspective, and attitude towards a 'can do' life! Whatever your goal is, Lisa can get you motivated and started on the right track by unleashing your inner power, YOUR POWER to succeed! She is truly an advocate for self discovery!

What I like most about interacting with Lisa is that she speaks from experience and speaks a language that can be understood by everyone from the everyday individual to the top researcher or scientist. There are no gimmicks or 'catches'. It's just a selfless endeavor that originates from one human being, Lisa, wanting you to be the very best you can be! Give it a shot! You won't be sorry.

Remember, one day, one conversation may not change your entire life—but it CAN and WILL get you started! Carpe Diem!"

~ Dr. Janice Collins,
Award-winning College Educator, Multi-Emmy Award-winning Journalist, and Motivational Speaker

 A HUMAN BEING

is part of the whole, called by us 'universe',

a part limited in time and space. He

EXPERIENCES HIMSELF,

his thoughts and feelings, as something separate

from the rest — a kind of optical delusion

of consciousness. This delusion is a kind of

prison for us, restricting us to our

PERSONAL DESIRES

and to affection for a few persons nearest to us.

Our task must be to FREE OURSELVES

from this prison by widening our circle of compassion to

EMBRACE ALL living creatures and the whole

of nature in its BEAUTY.

~Albert Einstein

FROM
BROKEN
TO
Beautiful

Lisa A. Hardwick

The author of this book does not dispense medical advice or prescribe the use of any technique as a form of treatment for physical or medical problems without the advice of a physician, either directly, or indirectly. If the reader chooses to use any of the information in this book, the author and publisher assume no responsibility for your actions.

BECKWORTH PUBLICATIONS

3108 E 10th St ~ Trenton, Mo 64683 ~ 660-204-4088

Ordering information: Quantity Sales. Special discounts are available on quantity purchases by corporations, associations, and others. For details, contact the "Special Sales Department at Beckworth Publications."

Beckworth Publications and the Beckworth Publications logo are trademarks of Beckworth Publications.

Printed in the United States of America.

Library of Congress Cataloging-in-Publication Data.

Hardwick, Lisa
From Broken to Beautiful : A Story of Brokenness Along with Life-Changing Discoveries and Strategies Applied to Create a Beautiful Authentic Life

Library of Congress Control Number: 2010916615

Cover Design: Mike Baugher
Senior Editor: Jack Hopkins
Content Assistant and Proof Executive Assistant: Haley York
Photographers: Kaitlin Lampley, Lisa Donahue
Interior Graphic Assistant: Giselle Rhuggenaath

CONTENTS

This book is

DEDICATED

to my amazing sons

Christopher Miller
Aaron Miller
Austin Miller

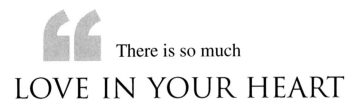 There is so much

LOVE IN YOUR HEART

that you could heal the entire planet.

But just for now let us

use this love to heal you.

~Louise L. Hay

ACKNOWLEDGEMENTS

I wrote this book for the children who lost their youth—both young and old and the many who have approached me who were in hope of learning more about my journey. I have seldom satisfied any listener with an abrupt answer or a short discussion over a quick cup of coffee at a local coffee house. By the time I am able to complete my story, we always seem to run out of time before the philosophy, the theories and the solutions were able to be presented and discussed. In essence, I suppose I wrote this book to have the ability to spread this gift of hope to more people than just the few who adamantly contacted me to schedule that third meeting at that coffee house to continue listening to the message.

People want hope. Almost everyone I have met along my journey is looking for peace, for purpose…and for hope. I found it, and when others realized I had…they always wanted to know more. My inner voice let me know on more than one occasion I was to write this book. It is the book I was supposed to write. You are holding it in your hands now.

I acknowledge with great joy and gratitude:

My mother, Linda Nugent. Without you this book would never have come to be. You and I "grew up together", didn't we? You were so young when I was born … You tell me daily how much you love me and how proud of me you are. Most of all you tell me how you believe in me. You have become the mother I was meant to have. Thank you for your love and support throughout this endeavor. Mom, I finally found ME. I'm home!

My stepfather, Monte Nugent. For the compassionate, supportive man you have become. Thank you for your support and openness to the philosophies for which I now live my life.

To my father. I know you did the best you could with the knowledge you had. I will always love you.

My eldest son, Christopher Miller. You always believed in me, son. You always thought I was the best mother in the universe, even when I was broken. May I now be the mother you deserve, today—and for the rest of your life.

My middle son, Aaron Miller. You always made me smile, just as you do today. Thank you for your unconditional love. Thank you for being you. May I now be the mother you deserve, today—and for the rest of your life.

My youngest son, Austin Miller. Always my little trooper. You tell me daily how wonderful a mother I am; thank you for your kindness, my little buddy. May I now be the mother you deserve, today—and for the rest of your life.

My brother, Cory Benge for taking me hiking up the mountain, which was another step in my healing journey. I am so proud of the man and the father you have become.

My nephew, Cashton Benge for giving me another reason to smile. For giving me another reason to always strive to be the best person I can be. You are a gift to Aunt Lisa, more than you could possible know.

Michelle Matteson, The Maven of the Mind for believing in me and for giving me your gift of amazing wind beneath my wings. I will always be grateful for your love and support. I further thank you for understanding about the need to write this book in my words to further assist me on my healing journey. I will always have a special place in my heart just for you.

Barbara Simmons, my oldest and dearest friend who was there with me during my brokenness and through the journey into my authentic beautiful life; you were there the day of my awakening, and I will always remember the strong, devoted, caring friend you were and are. You saw through the brokenness—you saw the diamond in the rough, and for that I will always be grateful for your love and friendship.

Lisa Donahue, also known as Chicago Mermaid for all that you are and all that you do, I thank you. You live the authentic life I believe most people aspire to. And to think I raised one eyebrow when I first learned your story—what a beautiful story it is! I look forward to the day when you are able to spread your message to the world. I want everyone to feel the way I have the privilege to feel when I am fortunate enough to spend the day with you. You are an amazing person.

Dr. William Boyd, who gave me hope and answered my millions of questions. If you have not heard anyone say "Thank You" in quite some time—then, Thank You, Dr. Boyd, for the vitally important work you do. I am grateful for you, your professionalism and your friendship.

Pastor Scott Sims, who prayed with me and for me. I will never forget that day in the coffee house when you encouraged me to write. Did you ever think your words would become so powerful? Thank you for your love. Thank you for being my pastor, my friend. Because of your encouragement, I now work diligently to make a difference in the lives of others utilizing my God-given gifts. Without understanding before, my past life was a gift to me; my future will be a gift to me…as well as to others.

Reggie Phillips for picking me up in that big old bus on that Wednesday night when I was nine years old…to introduce me to a "home" which I would later be able to find more easily because of your efforts.

Dr. Donald Donahue, who so graciously allowed me to utilize his beautiful retreat in Long Island, Bahamas where this book was finalized for release. You've raised the bar, Dr. Donahue, for I do not foresee being able to find a more beautiful setting anywhere else on this planet.

To all those I have hurt, I ask for your forgiveness.

To all those who have hurt me, I forgive you.

This book will never be classified as excellence in literacy, however it was written to assist and inspire others, to give hope and present a path that can lead to healing. It was written while laughing as well as through the blurred vision of tears. Most importantly, it was written with love.

LET THE HEALING BEGIN.

FOREWORD

From Broken to Beautiful is an astounding book that can serve as a life long guide to help lead you to healing, peace, transformation, and serenity. Even if you are not broken in spirit, you can benefit from this book because it speaks to every individual who may have been broken at one time in his or her life. It gives advice on how to achieve and maintain a healthy and balanced life so that you will understand and appreciate your inner beauty. People from all walks of life can relate to the author's voice, as she so humbly shares her own story. This book provides hope to so many that may be living a life of despair, a life of fear, or a life of just mere deception. If you have been broken in any of these or other areas of your life, you will learn how to move from broken to beautiful.

You will learn about topics such as the importance of forgiveness, the caution areas of relationships, and the understanding of prosperity and happiness. Layer by layer, line by line the author reveals key components to assist you on your journey.

The book is divided into three parts.

Self-Awareness:
The author uses the magic of self-awareness as the catalyst for opening new vistas of possibilities through focused intention, opening the heart, and making a contribution to others and the world at large.

Meditation and Exercises:
Thinking and reflecting on the content of each chapter in a structured left-brained manner that, in turn, will foster even more right brain creativity, you will be inspired through the use of various techniques as you learn exercises to enhance your mind, improve your body, and speak to your soul.

Transformation:
Through a story of self-revealing insights, you will discover new ways of transforming into who you were meant to become. Lisa Hardwick's insights allow virtually anyone from any background or traumatic past to say, "Ahh...I'm not alone; she did this, and I can too!" You will find hope as you read between the lines, and her story can become your story.

~ Dr. Mildred M. Pearson
Associate Professor
Eastern Illinois University

INTRODUCTION

 I remember that morning clearly. I was hoping the day would start no differently than the many other days experienced sporadically since my childhood. During these bouts of extreme panic, I had taught myself how to cope with the pain and severe anxiety attacks, and I would work very hard to make absolute certain that the secrets I was hiding would never be revealed. Yet on this particular morning the emotions were more painful than any other episode I have ever experienced. I now know what Hell feels like. I fell to my knees in front of the fireplace, forehead pressed hard against the floor in anguish, hands tightly clenched in fear. I painfully cried out, 'Today, I'm not going to make it!' I was exhausted, I was depleted, and I was unmasked. This particular morning, I had no choice but to surrender and give up all control. Something I never thought I could do, especially since I was such a control freak.

My greatest fear had come to be—I was broken.

Maybe you've experienced emotional pain such as this. Perhaps you have yet to experience this much pain, yet you are petrified a comparable morning could be right around the corner for you. Perhaps you are afraid that people are going to figure out that you wake up every morning feeling inadequate. That each day you feel like you don't fit in anywhere. Do you ever wish there was just someone somewhere who was very safe, a nonjudgmental God who you could discuss your life with and your thoughts about all that goes through your mind? Someone you could talk frankly to without being judged or punished? Thoughts such as: "I love my spouse, but I think it would be beautiful to have an affair with a passionate lover" or "how I hate my body" or "I am worried about my finances, yet I just bought a friend a gift I really can't afford" or "I just had a small pizza delivered and ate it all before I served grilled chicken salads to my family," "I had an affair," "I hate my job," "I just threw up my food."

Most people's greatest fear is that their secrets will be discovered, revealed, and they will become unmasked.

We are taught at an early age to live a fulfilled life; you had to have the nice home, impressive car, social status, job title, good income and a certain size waistline. So we go out to make our way into the world. We take the job we are expected to take, buy the home and car so all our friends and family will think we're successful, and we surround ourselves with the quality of people we feel we deserve. We marry the person for one reason or another, act a certain way, strive for particular goals—all the while worrying about our appearance, our ability to hang on to what we have and always looking for the next "thing" or "person" to make us happy.

Throughout all of this obtaining and developing we talk to ourselves terribly. "You are so fat!", "You can't do anything right!", "You never stick with anything!", "If my friends found out I was scared, they would leave me", "You don't really fit in—how long do you think you can keep this up?". Would you dare say these kinds of things to someone you care about? Then why would you say these things to yourself? Society has helped to condition us, and with this conditioning we will never measure up, not with the standards society has indicated we must reach. The home, career, relationships, social status, clothing size…all of these things we are supposed to accomplish are unattainable for any length of time. And if you happen to be one of those who DO achieve all that you are "supposed" to, it is extremely rare that you will be able to hold on to all of each expectancy for very long—and even if you do, it's still not a guarantee for a life of fulfillment and joy. Do you understand that all these expectancies and things we were taught to strive for are not natural?

We have programmed our minds to continue to play a tape recording of thoughts that focus on guilt, shame, resentment, competition, limits, illness, hardships and loss. From the earliest point of 'childhood-understanding' we're taught that you have to be smart to be worthy, you have to fit in, earn as much money as you can, you need to keep up with everyone, and doing it the "right way" is more important than loving yourself and loving others. We give so much credit to "things", like a car, a home, jewelry, clothes, our ego, our social status. We give no value to ourselves and others. We give no value to the very things that reciprocate our love. We carry these thoughts from childhood to our present, and the result is a life of fear. When we express fear it shows itself as pain, selfishness, addiction, disease, anger, ego, abusiveness, violence, fighting and war. We live an exhausting life living in fear. You can only go on for so long before you become physically tired, emotional and sad, you develop ailments, discomforts or many times diseases, and you go to the doctor for some "help".

It's highly likely you'll spend as little as ten minutes with your doctor before you are "diagnosed" with depression, a chemical imbalance, post traumatic stress syndrome, or perhaps the ever so popular "bipolar" disorder. Sound familiar? Perhaps you are one of those people who have yet to make the appointment with a doctor, but you've been thinking about it. Or maybe someone you know has been "diagnosed" by their doctor. It's pretty common and socially accepted now to speak freely about antidepressants that you or someone you know have been prescribed. We all know the latest popular antidepressants, don't we? Prozac, Zoloft, Wellbutrin, Paxil. You could probably chime off a half a dozen more names, couldn't you? As I sit and write this, my thoughts go to so many people I know and love and over half of them are on some kind of antidepressant. A few of my friends have said to me *"Yeah, but Lisa, the antidepressants work for ME!"* They must be one of the lucky ones because using traditional methods of treatment in this country have a .0005 recovery rate! Do you think their doctor let them know this when it was prescribed? And where does this disease of "depression" or "chemical imbalance" or whatever come from? It seems most of the people I know either "have it" or "have had it" in the past. How often do you believe a doctor is adamant about prescribing a personalize therapy program to get to the "root" of the problem in conjunction with the written prescription of anti-depressants? In my experience and others I have discussed it with - it's not often. I am not against taking anti-depressants. Yet I am concerned about the patient who thinks they are the sole source to "cure" their disease.

Let's say you are one who hasn't planned to visit your doctor or would never take an antidepressant prescription, yet you feel your life is so empty. You are filled with guilt, shame, resentment and/or perhaps anger. What are you doing to cope? Are you irritable and lashing out at people? Are you egotistical, always belittling others and perhaps bragging about *all* that you do and *all* that you have including how popular you are with *all* the "right people"? Are you a gossiper, always putting others down? Are you the comic of the group, making light of everything? Or are you the people pleaser? Ah, the people pleaser...always doing for others so you can "earn" your worthiness and acceptance. What about the person who blames everyone? It was their ex's fault, parent's fault, teacher's fault, *somebody's* fault. How are you making it through each day when deep inside you hate yourself and it seems everybody else has life figured out and you don't? Are you afraid that your days are numbered before some "one" or some "thing" removes your mask and it is revealed that you are now *broken*?

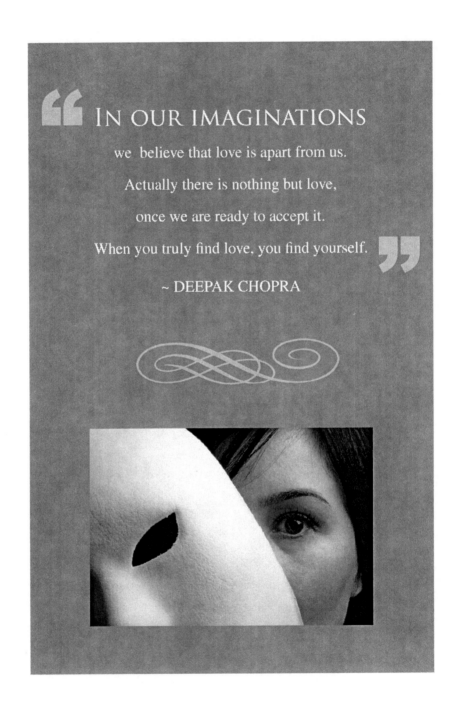

IN OUR IMAGINATIONS

we believe that love is apart from us.

Actually there is nothing but love,

once we are ready to accept it.

When you truly find love, you find yourself.

~ DEEPAK CHOPRA

Chapter 1

WHO ARE YOU?

Then I hear a voice. I intuitively know to be still and listen. So I listen, *really* listen and hear the voice coming from somewhere deep inside. The voice speaks slowly, yet clearly, *"You have been through enough, Lisa. I am here with you. Be patient."* I immediately respond with, *"What's happening? Oh, I get it, I've finally become mentally broken, a real nutcase, right?"* I lie still, desperate to hear this voice again and yet terrified because hearing voices means you are crazy, right? Isn't that what you would think? I knew the voice and words didn't come from my own thoughts. I was never that kind to myself. My own inner voice was harsh and filled with words of self-loathing.

But wait, the voice speaks again, loud and clear, *"You are okay, Lisa, and I promise everything is going to be fine. Get up now and be open to where I lead you. Trust me."* Rising from the floor, it seems as if I am watching all this happen from outside of my own body while a part of me still wonders, *"So is this what a mental breakdown feels like?"*

I head to the first shower in days, comforted by the warm water flowing over me. I don't know exactly what has happened, but one thing is certain...never from my earliest days have I felt such serenity and calm determination. No longer afraid of the voice, actually quite eager to experience it again, I am extremely curious to understand what exactly was happening inside my head. Was it a mental breakdown, the voice of God, or simply exhaustion laced with hallucination? What would you think?

Freshly showered and dressed, I marvel at my newfound determination to keep this new calm and to be open and aware of "the voice" should it happen to "speak" again. In fact, I decide it doesn't matter what the cause: a mental breakdown, a religious experience, exhaustion, whatever; all that matters is to experience "the voice" again. And I do! I bask in the wonderful feeling of calmness and clarity. I am able to concentrate when "the voice" shows up. The voice, I later found, was my gift of a very strong inner spirit into which I tapped during a *shift*, and it led me to many people, information, and instruction regarding the Body/Mind connection and Divine Spirit. Upon further research , I knew without a doubt whatever has been and might be broken will be beautiful. Beautifully broken and perfectly flawed.

How did becoming broken happen to me? To you? You may be wondering about the life events that led to my paralyzing emotional pain in front of the fireplace. Or perhaps you are nodding your head because you or someone you love is now living a life that is causing pain, certain behaviors, hopelessness, disease, paralyzing fear, or cynical defeat. Now some degree of emotional pain is a realistic part of life, isn't it? But, if you are reading this book, your pain or the pain of a loved one probably isn't the typical array of daily frustrations, is it? The suffering for which you seek answers more than likely has a long history or comes from an abrupt situation that is derailing life as you've always known it to be. Perhaps you, like me, sought or are now seeking relief in spending money, seeking one love partner after another, or overeating. Your story may have started in childhood, as mine did, which I carried throughout my entire life, or you are emerging from some sort of life trauma; perhaps you are currently in emotional pain or fear that pain is right around the corner. However or whenever your own suffering started, something made you choose this book. Pain is inevitable—you know this. Yet what is not inevitable is to be able to live a fulfilling, beautifully authentic life filled with joy in spite of life sufferings.

Constructing a timeline of my life from birth until that particular day in front of the fireplace was imperative to my healing. It was suggested by a certified professional whom I greatly respect. In this book, I am sharing a portion of my timeline, the good, the bad, the ugly, and the embarrassing moments. I am certain I have friends and family members reading up to this point thinking, *"Oh no, she didn't...did she?"* Well, the only way to heal is to "get real", and no one was more real than me when I created it. If you're not going to be honest about creating your timeline, don't even bother, it won't work. Perhaps sharing the "not so pretty" aspects of my personal timeline will help you to be able to relate to some of the sufferings, or perhaps your sufferings are quite different. Nonetheless, what doesn't change is pain that is felt and the havoc it creates. My personal belief is that suffering is allowed into our lives to refine us, to build character, and to force us to dig a little deeper into our soul. When I meet someone and notice that I am concentrating more on their behavior instead of the "person"—I recall my own timeline of pain and how I chose to cope before obtaining the tools to move from broken to beautiful. Constructing a timeline for yourself may help you to understand why you are now what you never wanted to be at this particular stage of your life.

The details of my own or your particular timeline are not as important as the lack of the tools in order to have a life of balance and joy AMID the suffering. I lived a life of regret, guilt, depression, and complete negativity, always searching for a means through another man, or another sales award, or food or alcohol to "fix" or "fill" me. What life are you living?

There were positive things that happened in my life throughout this timeline too: the birth of my three beautiful sons and watching them grow into smart, intelligent, productive young gentlemen, developing a wonderful relationship with my mother, the feeling of being valued by my stepfather, the birth of my adorable nephew, national sales awards, leadership recognition and other accomplishments. Yet, have you noticed that when you are so focused and expecting only painful things to happen, positive circumstances do not become readily available to you? And when they do, you don't really notice them, do you?

Today, I am very strong, aware, patient, emotionally balanced, spiritually healthy and live a life of joy. I have flaws and understand that perfection is impossible. Just knowing that perfection is unattainable is very freeing to me. My personal reinvention began on that particular morning on my knees, holding on for dear life in front of my fireplace. Where did yours begin? Not yet? Waiting to hear a "voice"? Maybe you just happened to see this book and "something" nudged you to pick it up. Was it random coincidence or a "voice"? You decide.

The gifts to recognize and utilize tools of reinvention were presented to me not by coincidence, but by "something" or "someone" more powerful than mere coincidence or luck. Coincidence doesn't happen day after day, week after week, year after year. And with these gifts also comes the responsibility to pass them on to you so that you and others like you may choose your own reinvention from broken to beautiful. A sense of fulfillment, peace, calmness and joy even on the days the size 12's are feeling tight, the self-talk is harsh, when everyone else's life seems more lucky, more competent, more beautiful than your own. Yes, you can still have a beautiful life. Maybe the bank account has dipped alarmingly, the spouse is cheating, the job is lost, foreclosure is imminent, the diagnosis is terminal or death has prematurely ripped a precious love from your life. You are still able to have a life of fulfillment, peace, calmness and joy…an authentically beautiful life.

Let me ask you something…who do you think you were created to be? Our spiritual beliefs may be different, probably are different, and that is okay. My belief is that God meant for me to be outgoing, creative, intelligent, witty and compassionate, and to lead a fulfilled, joyful and purposeful life. Many of these inborn traits were suppressed by my life circumstances, yet even more so by an inability of opportunity to obtain the necessary tools to regain balance when a life suffering incident would occur. Today, I feel it was a privilege to have lived the life I have lived. I feel I was trusted to endure life struggles without survival tools so that on that particular day in front of the fireplace I would be open to hear "that voice". I was trusted to be aware enough to seek tools to patch and repair the cracks of my life, and creative enough to put the methods I used into a format to assist others who find themselves "broken". I am so grateful for my transformation. I am equally grateful I am passing the newfound discoveries on to my own children who will then pass them on to their children. I am breaking the chain of past conditioning so when that new little person is born into my family, they will not have to endure the pain I experienced for over forty years. Perhaps you are a parent seeking these tools to repair a life gone flawed, and now in turn you want to be able to give your children these wonderful gifts so that if and when the child faces life suffering, they will be able to use the tools to still live a life of indescribable joy…an authentic, beautiful life.

OUR CONDITIONING

What we all are right now are victims of victims. With that said, remember, if you've been victimized—that person was acting the way they were taught. Their sense of judgement was off balance. They were doing the best they could. Wherever you are in life right at this particular moment is by all the conditioning, both negative and positive, that has taken place up until now. Conditionings come from your parents, relationships, teachers, society…and now even me. Can you imagine what the world would be like if it was mandatory that each child would learn what is REALLY important? If "REAL Life Skills" (and not the "Life Skills" taught in high school where we learn how to balance a check book, carry around an egg that is supposed to represent a baby and conduct an imaginary wedding) was a requirement the same as Math, Algebra, Science, and Language Arts? I'm telling you—we would heal the world!

What we all are right now are victims of victims.

I am not a healer. I think of myself as a road to your self-discovery. You can take any road—you just happen to be traveling down the road I put a billboard up on, and you are curious to take a closer look, wondering if this might be the road for you because, *"She obviously has it figured out, and I want what she has."* And for those of you who have been introduced to the many I have assisted with *their* journey, you probably have noticed how much more healthy and vibrant they look, you realize they love themselves, they have the financial flow they need, their relationships are wonderfully different, their careers flourish and their lives keep getting better. I truly believe in my heart that my gift to the Universe, my purpose for being born, is to give you the gift of self-discovery. The gift of You! Amazing, talented, purposeful You!

A HUNDRED BUCKS

A *hundred bucks*. A hundred bucks is what it cost for the additional weight of the large suitcase I was checking in at the airlines. I didn't care—I would have paid twice that amount—I was determined this suitcase was going with me on my trip with my mother to Montana.

My mother had been worried about me for quite some time long before I heard "the voice". And she became very concerned, observing my increasingly alarming and life-altering changes that I tried in the desperate hope one of them was the magic quick fix. Was it another diet this time or another husband? Was I going to build a new home, or was it going to be another trip to the doctor for another magic pill? My mother said she knew it was not a question of if, but when I would hit rock bottom again. I did hit bottom, sure that the voice I had heard so clearly was nothing more than "me finally going crazy" and that my life was truly broken beyond repair.

Mom was determined to help when she offered to fly with me to Montana to visit my brother and his little boy, whom we both adored. Still numb with yet again paralyzing emotional pain when she presented the itinerary to me, I suddenly felt, rather than heard, "the voice", and once again as before, felt an instant calm yet fierce determination to change my situation once and for all. It was obvious that my way wasn't working. My life was a mess again. I couldn't hide it anymore. I didn't have the energy to hide it. Before, I had the energy to make a mess of my life, then make a geographical move and start a new life. I always had the outgoing personality to make new friends and act as if I had it all together. I attracted the kind of friends I felt I deserved—and since I hated myself, you can imagine that the "friends" I developed relationships with were just as broken and most of the time more so. Relocating again was not an option this time.

What was the difference between this crystal moment of "the voice" and the one in front of the fireplace? What was the difference between this vow to "try" to change and all the others of my past? Belief. I believed as sure as I was breathing that I was on the edge of a new awakening and I was more than ready to leap.

Over the past twenty years, in the quest for relief from my pain, I had purchased enough of every type of self-help book, manual, CD, DVD, book on tape and podcast and you-name-it program to fill a small library—most lay unread, as if the act of buying would somehow turn my life around—after all "buying was trying, wasn't it?" I packed all that could be stuffed into the large suitcase along with two new journals and my laptop; hence the hundred bucks in luggage fees. I was on a healing mission. I knew in my heart, more than I had ever felt before, that I was going to figure this out. I had always been an over pleaser when it came to accomplishing goals set for me by others for their own gain as my attempt to show my value. This time, it was for me.

My brother's home is beautiful, spacious and surrounded by the wondrous Montana Mountains. Yet, it wouldn't have mattered where I was. I was going to figure this out even if it meant spending a week in a lousy hotel room in the middle of a destitute town. I studied for seven days and most of every night, barely sleeping, taking a few moments for meals, devoting hours of time to study, taking notes, researching and developing a plan to reinvent my life— to become beautiful instead of broken. I was surprised at my ability for focused intensity, how I seemed to just know what to research and where to find it and how I was experiencing extreme peacefulness throughout this time.

Seven days later I understood more than I had from all my years of visiting treatment centers . I now understood what was needed for reinvention and I knew with this new knowledge I would never be the same. I would later become educated as a certified teacher in these newfound discoveries. The desire to achieve this reinvention was the strongest emotion I had ever experienced in my life but even more so than desire—I believed I would achieve reinvention. I KNEW IT! *This* time, I was divinely guided. Through following the guidance of my inner voice, I transformed my life, and you can too…one day, one hour, one moment at a time.

There are many self-help tools on the market, and I began a mission to study and research most of them with the assistance of psychologists, sociologists, pastors and certified professionals. I was confident. I had already started putting some of my outline into practice and literally began feeling small, positive changes. Even the smallest of changes was exciting. Each day my belief grew stronger as I developed an amazing consciousness, dissolved barriers, tapped into my own inner spirit, learned more about self-love and forgiveness of others as well as myself. I've spent more years being "sick" than I've been "healthy", and I have a lot of making up to do on this journey for myself. I deserve it. I continue to strive for wholeness every day. I don't claim to be perfect. I'm human. But I do claim to work on the gifts that were presented to me each and every day. I am so excited knowing that in helping you I will continue to heal and grow as well. I've already surpassed my expectations for reinvention, for healing, so the rest of my life is spent waking up every morning, centering myself before my feet touch the floor and being excited about what miraculous things I am going to experience that day. I want this for you too.

Reflections FOR CHAPTER 1

Now that I look back at those initial days of my recovery, of my transition from broken to beautiful, I can see an undercurrent of feelings and thoughts that contributed in a holistic manner to the person I am today. The calmness, the self-belief, the peace and the faith to go on...these are virtues that can alter your thoughts and lead you on the path to a healthy body, mind and soul.

I know that these qualities do not become imbibed within you in a day. And not having a voice to guide you can make it all the more difficult, though not impossible. How can you make calmness, peace, hope and self-belief a part of your life? How can you help yourself wake up each day with a smile, knowing that life is good no matter what trials or travails you have to face?

Here's a meditation technique I find very effective, and you might too. A few minutes each day spent on this technique can make a huge difference in how the rest of your day goes. Called the Stillness Meditation, it is probably the easiest to master and can bring calm and peace to otherwise harried lives.

STILLNESS MEDITATION:

Before You Begin:

1. Ensure that the place you choose to meditate within is quiet and comfortable with as few distractions as possible.

2. Do a few stretching exercises.

The Actual Technique:

1. Sit down on the floor or on a chair in a position you find comfortable.

2. Close your eyes and inhale. As you breathe in, tense up your limbs, neck and face. Focus on the stillness when you tense up.

3. Slowly exhale and release the tension. As you exhale, try to imagine all your thoughts moving out of your mind.

4. Go through the steps slowly. Take a moment after each exhalation to savor the calmness that flows into you. Do this for ten minutes each day to make calmness a part of you.

Remember, you'll master the technique as time goes by. Persevere in your quest for peace, hope and all things good and they'll come to you!

Notes

Notes

Notes

Notes

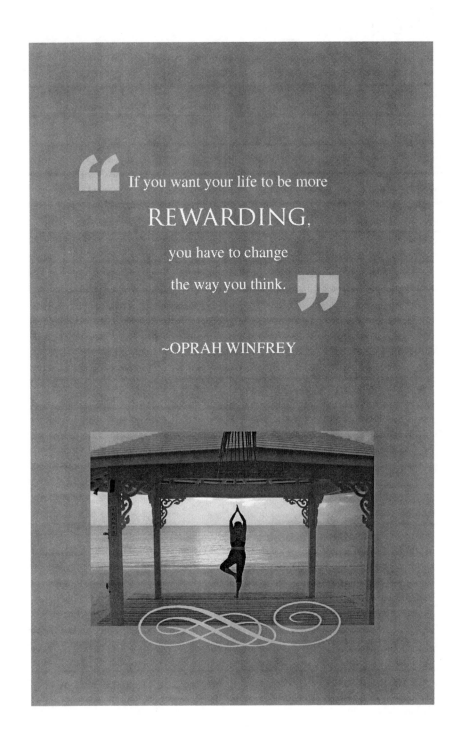

If you want your life to be more

REWARDING,

you have to change

the way you think.

~OPRAH WINFREY

Chapter 2

YOUR REMARKABLE MENTAL AUTHORITY

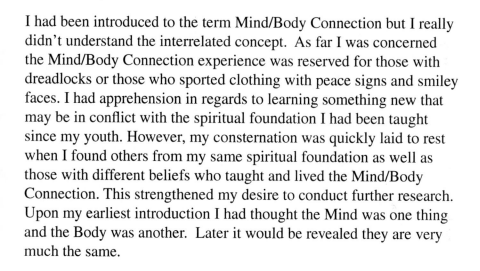

I had been introduced to the term Mind/Body Connection but I really didn't understand the interrelated concept. As far I was concerned the Mind/Body Connection experience was reserved for those with dreadlocks or those who sported clothing with peace signs and smiley faces. I had apprehension in regards to learning something new that may be in conflict with the spiritual foundation I had been taught since my youth. However, my consternation was quickly laid to rest when I found others from my same spiritual foundation as well as those with different beliefs who taught and lived the Mind/Body Connection. This strengthened my desire to conduct further research. Upon my earliest introduction I had thought the Mind was one thing and the Body was another. Later it would be revealed they are very much the same.

HOW OUR LIVES ARE SHAPED

After much research, speaking with certified professionals, accredited physicians and taking specialized classes—I learned the Mind/Body Connection in a nutshell is about how our thoughts create our lives, including our physical health. My life during this research was still a mess, but I knew I was learning valuable information. I had been diagnosed with severe clinical depression, post traumatic stress syndrome, and morbid obesity. All the ways I used to numb pain were no longer working—you know, the food, the relationships, the prescriptions as well as a few other methods, depending on my mood at that time.

*Our thoughts create our lives,
including our physical health.*

The more I read about the Mind/Body Connection, the more hopeful I became. When I learned that the body responds to the way you think, feel and act, I was like, *"Well, no wonder I've been depressed and obese most of my life!"* When your emotional health is out of balance, physical signs such as the following may show up to alert you:

~ Weight Gain   ~ Weight Loss
~ Headaches   ~ Back Pain
~ Stiff Neck   ~ Acne
~ Constipation   ~ Diarrhea
~ Loss of Energy   ~ Cancer
~ Migraines   ~ Increase of Appetite
~ Depression   ~ Anorexia
~ Ulcers   ~ Blurred Vision

There can be multiple physical ailments, discomforts and diseases as a result of your thoughts. After gaining this knowledge, I determined that if our thoughts really do affect our life, our peace and our health, I could really change my life once and for all.

"AH HA" MOMENTS

A couple of "ah ha" moments for me while I was in the beginning stages of learning about the power of the mind happened during another trip I took to visit my brother in Montana. My brother, Cory Benge, is very athletic and he bases an enormous amount of importance on his health, including his daily exercise and nutrition. I, on the other hand, had never been athletic besides an occasional stroll to the stop sign at the end of the street and back while most often losing my breath at the halfway mark. That "stroll plan" had a commitment stage that lasted sometimes three days at the most.

I usually make a few trips a year from my home in Illinois to Montana to simply help my brother who is a single parent. A typical visit consists of Cory picking me up from the airport and taking me to his home where I clean, cook, shop for their needs (ok, ok, things my *nephew* needs like toys…lots of toys), redecorate a few rooms, cook a Thanksgiving Dinner or put up their Christmas tree, buy and wrap presents, and the best part of all, take care of and play with my nephew. One evening during this particular visit, Cory told me we are going to go hiking up a mountain the next day. Just Cory, my little nephew, who was about three years old at the time, and myself. I figured if my nephew could hike, then just maybe I could do it too, yet, even though I didn't tell my brother, I was terrified because I was in very poor physical shape and I was fairly certain I would not be able to enjoy this activity the way he seemed so certain I would.

That night after I put my nephew to bed, I climbed the stairs to my room and I could feel the stinging of the tears emerging stronger with each step. *"I don't want to go hiking tomorrow. What if I can't do it! What if my brother gets upset with me and rolls his eyes and I ruin the entire day for everyone!"* I was certain I would be anxious for the rest of the night and probably wouldn't even sleep. I was scared. I didn't want to let myself down. I didn't want to embarrass myself in front of two people I love. I didn't want to disappoint my brother.

Even as I write this, I weep for the woman who was climbing those stairs. The woman who always put herself down and was so worried about disappointing everyone. The woman who would numb her pain with food or perhaps another new relationship. The woman who always thought she deserved men who would dismiss her and roll their eyes. The woman who was exhausted by being a people pleaser to everyone so she could "earn" her worth. I thank God every day I am no longer that woman.

The brain cannot process fear and gratitude at the same time.

I got into bed that night and turned on the little lamp on the nightstand. I picked up one of the many books I had brought about the mind, or the brain, or science. I was so fearful about the next day I didn't even know if I would be able to concentrate. I opened my randomly chosen book to no particular marked place and read something to the affect, "The brain cannot process fear and gratitude at the same time. All negative emotions are fear based, so if you want to eliminate fear in your life, meditate on all you are grateful for...." I had read this many times before in a variety of books regarding science and the brain. Yet that night, God opened that book to exactly where I needed to read. I put some soothing music on my iPod, turned out the lights and started thinking about all that I was grateful for. *My sons, my parents, my brother and nephew, my friends, my awareness of my past conditioning and my commitment to heal for myself and those I love...*Every so often a thought or a vision would enter my mind that was a "put down" or of someone from my past who had hurt me or who I had hurt, and I would ever so gently acknowledge it and think...*I acknowledge you, and I am going to send you away, and if you come back to my thoughts while I am focusing on all that*

I am grateful for, I will continue to acknowledge you are there then gently push you away.... After a while of meditation and breathing and focusing my thoughts on all I was grateful for, my fear was gone, completely vanished. I lay there with a slight smile on my face as I drifted off to a peaceful sleep while dreaming of all I was grateful for.

The next morning I was awakened by my little nephew who was so excited about the day. We made breakfast together, got dressed in our hiking gear and made our way to the mountain. Once in the parking lot of our destination, my brother began putting on his "hiking papoose" to carry my nephew within it. The combined weight of the carrier we named the "hiking papoose" and my nephew would mean my brother would be hiking this gigantic mountain with over 80 lbs strapped to his back. My brother explained there are two ways to hike up the mountain...straight up or diagonal. We took the diagonal, which had eight "switchbacks". This way was less difficult yet much longer because you would go back and forth across the mountain. The other way had sections, looked like it was straight up when viewing it from the ground and was a much more difficult way to climb. I noticed the few people who were on it looked like advanced professional athletes. We were preparing to hike the less difficult, longer way of course because, well, you know the story about my stroll to the stop sign and back. Cory allowed my nephew to start the hike without being confined to his back in the "papoose". The little guy knew exactly where to go as he began to climb the first switchback trail with what seemed little effort *(it certainly seemed this way since he was running at full speed and laughing!)*. My brother and I laughed at his already developed athletic ability. He was most certainly a chip off the old block.

We were about halfway up the first switchback when it happened. I couldn't breathe. Cory and my nephew were quite a bit ahead of me, yet I could see them. I started having what felt like a panic attack, and my chest started to restrict. I found the strength to call out "Cory!" He didn't hear me. "Cory!" I tried desperately again. I continued to look his way and watch him. He was preoccupied, keeping a close eye on his son while maneuvering his own self up the steep trail. He finally glanced back and saw me. He called to my nephew, and I watched as they both effortlessly ran back to where I was standing. I felt defeated. I was embarrassed. My negative thought conditioning was taking over, and it was winning.

"You okay, sis?" he asked.

"I can't do it. I can't breathe. My lungs won't fill with air," I replied while my eyes filled with tears. My thoughts went to, *"I'm such a loser. All those times of overeating, lying around, smoking cigarettes and being a complete loser are ruining everyone's day. A three year old can run up this mountain, and I think I need to quit at only halfway up the first switchback trail. Hell, I'm just destined to be a fat, morbidly obese, depressed woman who has no talent and will always come in last. I'm so different than anyone else."*

For the first time in our adult lives, my brother looked me in the eyes and said, "Well, first of all, you need to stop talking to yourself that way. You CAN do this. Your thoughts are the key to anything you can or cannot accomplish. Second of all, we WILL make it up this mountain even if it takes all day. Third, hold your arms like this and breathe. This will fill your lungs with air."

I did as he told me to, and I began to feel a little better, but a part of me still just wanted to quit and go back to the car. We started up the switchback trail again before I could tell him I thought I wanted to quit and that I'd changed my mind. This time we went much slower while my nephew was right by my side and my brother on my other side, reminding me to talk to myself. *"I can make it up this mountain."*

He said, "Even if you don't believe it, say it anyway."

My nephew looked up and across me to my brother. "Are we going slow because of Aunt Lisa?"

My brother and I both laughed out loud.

My nephew continued, "It's okay, Aunt Lisa, you can do it!"

For the first time in my life, I didn't see my brother as a little brother. He was a wise adult man. Did he always know how do to this—how to think like this? I always figured it came naturally to him. That it was just a part of his genetic makeup and I missed out on those particular genes. Perhaps he got what I was supposed to have. Yet remembering my research, someone had to teach him. These weren't the thoughts he or I were conditioned to have. Something or someone in his past assisted him with this power through their positive conditioning in this area. Perhaps it was a former football coach, or a college professor or a hunting buddy.

One day I was having a discussion with a friend of mine, Lisa Donahue, explaining how my brother and I had lived the same childhood and I could not understand why I turned out the way I did—and he didn't.

She looked at me and spoke with her gentle voice. "You didn't live the same lives. You were brought into this world under completely different circumstances. Your parents were at a different age and maturity level when you were each born. You were not the same gender. You had different experiences, both positive and negative, in which you were both conditioned differently. You most certainly did not have the same childhoods. You have developed your coping skills, both healthy and unhealthy, and he has developed his own coping skills, both healthy and unhealthy. You both have always done the best that you could, but you most certainly have not lived the same lives."

She was right. I had never thought about it that way. That day on the mountain, my brother shared with me one of his healthy coping skills, and for this, I am grateful and I couldn't be more proud of him for practicing such positive thought processes, for himself, for his son, for me. This was just another stepping stone to my clarity—to my self-discovery.

Hiking up the trails became more difficult. My brother told my nephew it was time to get in the "papoose". Of course my nephew showed us he was very upset about this by pursing his little lips and crossing his arms, but he did it anyway. He was promised he would be able to see the view so much better, and I encouraged him to tell me about all that he saw. I kept talking to myself, *"You can make it up the mountain. You can make it to the top."*

There were areas within the switchbacks that were straight up. When we would get to those particular places, my brother knew what would more than likely go through my thoughts. He yelled out at me with a grin, "Now before you start talking yourself out of it, let me tell you how to do this." I watched him as he put his "fingers in this cranny" and his "left foot on this tiny ledge" while his "right hand grabbed a root over there" and hoisted himself up to the next level. Remember, he had a toddler and 80lbs on his back and a sister who suffered from low self-confidence that he was most likely thinking about.

It was now my turn. I said to myself, *"I can do this. There is a way to do this, and I am going to listen to his instructions and get up this cliff!"* And I did. And I was proud. And I was slowly gaining some self-assurance and self-confidence. I laugh now as I think about looking up one of the cliffs at my brother who was giving me instructions as to what to do next, and saw him bending over with his hands on his knees looking down at me while I looked directly above him and noticed my nephew in the "papoose". His head was above my brother's with his little elbows on my brother's shoulders, and he was resting his cheeks in his own miniature hands. His little body language looked as if he was saying, *"I'm so bored. Jeesh, come on. Don't you realize this is fun? It's not fair I have to sit up here in this 'papoose' while you get to climb this cliff."*

We reached the seventh switchback, and it was more difficult than anything I had ever tried physically or athletically, which wasn't much. My brother told me to give him my arm, and he tucked it under his massive, muscular bicep and practically pulled and dragged me up to almost the top.

"We're almost there, Sissy," he encouraged me. "We're almost to the top!"

Right before the top, Cory released my arm, which allowed me to make my own way to the top of this mountain. I stopped and overlooked the city of Bozeman, Montana and felt an exhilaration I will never forget. My thoughts, my very own thoughts, though guided with the assistance of my brother and encouragement from my nephew, got me to the top of this mountain. I stood in awe of all that I had learned thus far on my healing journey.

We all began to make our way back down the mountain which, though still difficult, was much easier than hiking up. When we had just a couple of switchbacks to go, Cory let my nephew out of his carrier and let him run alongside of him to the bottom. I took my time to avoid falling and laughed while I watched my toddler nephew seem "to hold his own" with his dad.

Down the last switchback, my nephew cheered me on, smacking his little hands on his upper legs, yelling, "Come on, Aunt Lisa, you're almost there, you can do it!" obviously amusing the bystanders with his genuine enthusiasm.

As we met at the bottom, my brother instructed me to go ahead and take my nephew home and he would meet up with us later. Cory let me know he was going to "run" up the mountain again on the difficult side.

"Are you kidding me?" I asked him.

"No, I try to do it every day," he replied.

I strapped my nephew in his car seat and began driving to the opening of the parking lot, but then my intuition told me to turn back around. I was just learning to trust my intuition, so I turned the car around and parked in an area where I could see the difficult sections up the mountain. There I watched my brother running, digging in his hiking shoes, arms pumping back and forth, muscles flexing, breathing hard. But do you know what I saw that was more awesome than anything? I saw my younger brother, my brother who was now a man to me, talking to himself. He talked to himself while he passed other athletic hikers and runners, over roots and large rocks that were in his path, right up that mountain. His mountain. My mountain. Your mountain.

If the mind tells you that you can, you can.

I have learned if someone has the physical ability to climb a mountain but doesn't have the mental ability, they won't make it to the top. And I also learned if someone has the mental ability but doesn't necessarily have the physical ability, they can STILL make it to the top. Today, I have learned so much about the body and mind, how the mind works, and I have made tremendous strides from that day on that mountain. Today, I have the ability to make it to the top of any mountain I choose, whether it be in Montana, in my office or whatever "mountain" just so happens to be presenting itself in my life.

Reflections
FOR CHAPTER 2

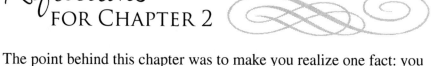

The point behind this chapter was to make you realize one fact: you can make yourself do whatever you want if you can train your mind to think you can. Your mind is not a malleable little thing sitting housed there within your skull. It can often function as an entity unto itself, and I've experienced it often enough. It can make you see things that aren't there, it can make you believe in things that aren't true, it can take you to the depths of depression and it can bring you to the pinnacle of success.

The amount of affect your mind has upon you depends on the amount of affect you *let* it have. You've seen how my mind talked to me before I learned to control it. It is how minds generally talk. The trick is learning how to control it, to make it see what you want it to see, to believe what you want it to believe and to take you to the zenith and beyond.

So how can you control your mind? You need two things in order to be the winner in this struggle for control: faith and steadfastness. Have you noticed how if you keep telling yourself "I can do it!" often enough, you start believing it? That's because you succeed in drowning your mind's useless, discouraging chatter. "When you can't beat them, join them" is your mind's policy. When it can no longer make you do its bidding, it helps you along your path of thinking… towards success.

Here are simple things you can do to let your mind know who the boss is. They simply involve not doing what your mind tells you to:

1. There are dishes to be washed and you feel lazy. Don't postpone! Override your mind and go and do it. NOW!

2. Do you like sugar in your coffee? Have coffee without sugar for a week. You might feel like adding a little sugar each time you hold a coffee. Don't, that's your mind talking.

3. You might come home from work and plop yourself in front of the TV. Get up and go have a shower instead.

4. When you start having negative feelings or thoughts, know that it's your mind working towards discouraging you. Realize the futility of these thoughts and dismiss them. Don't give your mind any ammunition against you.

You can try overcoming the influence of your mind in every way you want. Doing this often enough will convince you and your mind that you'd only do things *you* want to do and not what your mind wants you to. *You* have control!

Notes

Notes

Notes

Notes

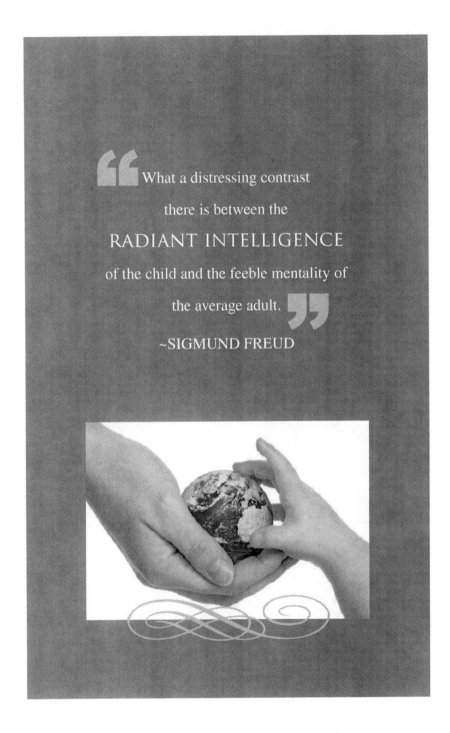

> What a distressing contrast there is between the **RADIANT INTELLIGENCE** of the child and the feeble mentality of the average adult.
>
> ~SIGMUND FREUD

Chapter 3

THE CHILD WITHIN

We have all heard them before. *"Let the past go, and move on. The past is the past, leave the past behind."* I agree to some degree. But to let the past go, we need to acknowledge what the negative part of the past is so we are able to let that particular part go. Otherwise, we just try to numb that memory that may be filled with pain, remorse, resentment, guilt, shame, etc. in many different ways, such as through discomfort, pain, disease, depression or ailments.

Let the past go, and move on.

Many people would claim "it's just too hard" to go back in the past and bring up all those unpleasant painful memories and deal with them. They claim they are much too busy. Well, do you think they are too busy when they have no energy and cry themselves to sleep again? Or do you think they are too busy when they have to drive themselves three hours away for another chemotherapy treatment? Do you think they are too busy when they have to wait for one of their friends to pick them up and drive them to the chiropractor's office because they are so tense from the stress they are under that their back is out again? Believe me, if I can go back and face the pain in my past, I know you are able to go back as well. I have met people on my journey who had more past pain than I could ever fathom, and once they worked through it, they became some of the strongest, most vibrant people you would ever know. They now thrive in life. Just like me. Just like you will.

Negative messages from our youth are stored in our Inner Child

Do you ever wonder where many of the negative messages from our youth are stored? They are stored in our Inner Child. These messages are the ones that place limits on our thinking. It is of vital importance to your emotional healing to get in touch with the part of your Inner Child who feels lonely, scared, unloved, perhaps lost, rejected and doesn't feel they were worth much. How do you talk to your Inner Child today? Do you put it down? Yell at it? Criticize it? No wonder we are so unfulfilled and unhappy. Your Inner Child is a part of You. We can't talk poorly to the child within and expect to be in balance, complete and whole.

YOUR CHILDHOOD HISTORY TIMELINE

I remember the first time I was asked to make my childhood's history timeline in a group. My family was always amazed by my ability to remember so much of my earliest days in childhood. Most of the people in my group consisted of educated people with high credentials, including PhD's, and about half of those couldn't remember the years before they were five years old. Our instructor informed us this was quite natural and to simply start with birth, write how we felt we were greeted when we came into the world the moment we left the birthing canal, and then start labeling the years with the memories that we were able to remember. I remember when my Uncle John tried to help my grandma change my diaper on her bathroom floor. He was having a heck of a time and Grandma laughed about that little event for years. He must have been about 14 years old and I must have been between 12–18 months old.

The short version of my childhood timeline went as follows:

Birth: I know I was not planned . I was born to 16 year old parents who were scared to death. I had heard the first thing my dad cried out when he saw me was, "Oh God, she is so ugly!" The family laughed and talked about that for years. Later, when I was a teenager my father told me that the only reason I was here was because my mother became pregnant to "trap" him because she knew he was interested in dating someone else. The truth is, he forced her to have sex and she became pregnant.

One–Two Years: Just a few memories of lying in my crib and my Uncle John trying to change my diapers. To this day he and I still laugh about it when we see each other.

Two–Three Years: I remember my brother being brought home from the hospital, and being laughed at and dismissed when I sat down on the living room floor like a "good girl" and asked if I could hold him.

I remember having my picture taken and exactly where I was and sometimes even what I was wearing.

I remember putting up a Christmas tree.

I remember riding my little horse, Patches, and a gentleman on a large horse spooking it and my father running after the horse. I remember his half zipper boots running towards me while I hung upside down and later let go before the horse trampled me. I remember it took days to pull the rocks out of my scalp.

Four-Five Years Old: I remember the "games" I played with an adult. This manipulation and sexual abuse went on for many years.

 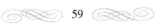

Fast forward

Eight–Ten Years Old: I remember my favorite grandmother dying at a very young age while she was napping on her couch, my parents divorcing, moving to another home and another trusted adult sexually abusing me. I remember hearing the word obesity for the first time. I remember my other grandmother who I loved very much said I was no longer her granddaughter because my parents divorced. I remember my father "forgetting" to pick up my brother and I for visits. I remember being very scared because we were left alone while my mother was at work and I was responsible for the care of my little brother. I remember sitting at the front door with a butcher knife to "protect" my little brother should anyone try to break in and hurt us.

The timeline I actually conducted in class took hours to complete. Yet the shortened version will give you an idea of some of the things I remembered. Until this exercise, I hadn't realized how filled I was with such painful memories. I felt two emotions as I wrote...those emotions as a child and also those emotions as an adult. The child's emotions were filled with guilt, shame, resentment, remorse and pain. The adult's emotion was filled with compassion, sympathy and heartfelt love. Never in my wildest dreams had I ever experienced such a mass of emotions as I did during this exercise.

Allow me to introduce you to … little you.

Upon writing your own childhood's history timeline, be gentle with yourself. Put on some soothing music and relax. Then write from your heart to your pen. Do not think about what you will be writing; no one needs to see this unless you want to share with someone you trust. Upon the completion of this exercise, comfort the child throughout your timeline. Think about sitting the child on your lap, talking to her/him, soothing her, talking to her with mature, safe love.

You carry this child around with you throughout your day, every day, 24/7.

For example: I meditate on being brought into this world. The day I was born, I picture myself running over to the baby, picking her up gently. Marveling at how beautiful she is! Wrapping her in a warm blanket and holding her close as I kiss her little hands. *"You are so beautiful! Life has so many wonderful adventures for you! Everyone is so happy you are here!"*

As I would meditate on each child in my timeline—many times I would have a picture of myself around the particular age I was focusing on that I could look at while I was doing the exercise. The picture I found of myself at the age of 10 years old I enlarged to an 8 x 10. When it came off the color copier, I looked at this child and dropped to my knees and wept for her. She had been through so much, and I had carried that pain around with me for all these years. Healing my inner child was one of the most important life changing discoveries and strategies I practiced on my healing journey to my transformation. Yes, it was a painful process, yet it was more painful to carry around that beaten down 10 year old than to go through the painful process and be released. Once released, I felt a hundred pounds lighter. It was if my body was full of light inside. I still carry around a couple of pictures of myself from my childhood. Every once in a while, if I have a moment such as waiting at the airport, or in line at the grocery story, I pull out one of the pictures just to reconnect with her—for whatever amount of time I might have to spend with her—just so she knows I am "here" and will always be here for her.

What I have come to understand for myself after completing the exercise is that even though I experienced an abundance of healing through that particular strategy, it is most certainly beneficial to continue to comfort and heal my inner child as a part of my ongoing journey.

I recently attended a workshop in San Diego, California for training of Certified Teachers and Leaders for the Heal Your Life® Workshops and Seminars. These workshops were created and conducted by Dr. Patricia Crane and her husband, Rick Nichols, through their company Heart Inspired Presentations, LLC. Heart Inspired Presentations, LLC is authorized by Hay House, Inc. and approved by Louise Hay. They have been teaching these principles internationally for years and wrote their own book called Cosmic Kitchen. Dr. Patricia Crane worked directly with Louise Hay as an assistant to her in workshops. As Hay House, Inc. grew, Louise began turning her attention more toward the book publishing business while Dr. Crane just naturally picked up the mantle and continued with the teachings. Both Dr. Crane and Rick Nichols are two of the most respected and talented teachers of healing I have ever been honored to work with. During this particular workshop, they taught us how to do their program's Inner Child healing exercise. Even though I had already completed a considerable amount of work in this area, the exercise was amazing.

The meditation started with asking us all to close our eyes, relax our bodies and see ourselves as a little child of about five. We were to welcome our little child and say, "I am your future and I have come to love you." The meditation continued with us embracing this child with love and bringing this child with us to our present time. As we and this child stand together, we become aware of many parts of us that are missing. The meditation takes us to all of those parts from birth, to when we took our first steps, our first day of school, about the age of ten (this was a very intense moment for me), puberty, teenage years, our first job, our first love, our first milestone. The meditation took us through embarrassing, confusing, painful as well as wonderful and joyous moments. It continued all the way through to our future self. Yes, our future self. And it was a glorious adventure.

All you are today, and all your strengths, weaknesses, and destructive behaviors, are a major part of your development. If we were nurtured and cared for and properly guided in each of our developmental phases, such as infant to toddler, elementary to teenager, then we are most likely to grow into a balanced, emotionally healthy adult. But that is many times not the case. Wouldn't you agree? I remember during one of my speaking engagements, I asked everyone to close their eyes and then asked them to raise their right arm and stretch it high above their head. After a few moments I gently asked, "Who has parent issues?" And everyone laughed. I laughed as well. I then asked if everyone would please keep their eyes closed and their hand in the air and seriously asked them to slowly put their hands down if they had no parental issues such as resentment, anger, shame, etc. There were very few who put their hands down. In fact, I only noticed two who claimed they did not have any issues, and there were probably close to three hundred who most certainly did. This revealed to me that there is much work to be done in our society. We most certainly need to go back and heal that child within.

Those unresolved painful things that hurt us so much when we were children show themselves in our relationships today, including the relationship with ourselves.

We may be showing the unresolved pain by being in unhealthy relationships or abusive relationships. We may not have learned about boundaries. We may have addictions to food, alcohol or drugs. Perhaps low self-esteem. Unresolved pain from childhood can rear its ugly head in many forms into our adult lives.

 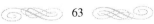

I believe when you begin to understand the power of the pain of the inner child, it seems to make you more compassionate not only to yourself, but to others as well. I notice people every day who most likely are struggling with some kind of unresolved pain. And now I am certain you will too. Be gentle with them. Be gentle with yourself. Remember, we were doing the best we could with the experience and care we were given. This is especially healing for victims of childhood sexual abuse. I've witnessed firsthand the transition from victim to healthy survivor practicing tools of healing for the inner child.

LOVE *is what we were born with.*
FEAR *is what we learned here.*

~MARIANNE WILLIAMSON

Reflections FOR CHAPTER 3

Now that you've read some exercises you could do to help you connect with your inner child, why not do them? No matter how good and protected your upbringing, there must have been some time in your childhood when you felt insecure, unloved or scared. You might have relegated that experience to the dark recesses of your mind and may not even remember it now, but it's there, and you do not know the amount of influence it probably has on your day-to-day life.

Similarly, no matter how troubled and unloved your upbringing was, there must have been some time in your childhood when you smiled, laughed, felt happy and secure.

Here are some simple things you can do to help your inner child (and ultimately the adult you) overcome the sadness that plagued it in the past and live happily like it did in those moments of security and love:

1. ***Make a Journal:*** Writing down your pains, fears, hopes and desires helps…a lot! Start a journal, title it "(Your Name)'s healing journey" and write everything you remember from your childhood. Feel the child's pains, fears and hopes as you write. As an adult, go to the child and ease its fears, make it feel secure. Each time you remember a painful incident and write it down in the journal, work towards easing the pain you felt then. Reconnect with the small you, with the child you were. Do NOT look at it from your adult perspective. If you remember the time you got lost in a garden and were feeling scared, do not dismiss the incident, thinking from the adult's perspective that you weren't really lost and your parents were right there in the garden. Remember the child you were at that point in time, the fears you had. Connect to and relive those fears and insecurities. Then approach your inner child as an adult and coddle and love it and assure it of its safety.

2. ***Write two letters:*** Write a letter to your inner child, soothing its fears, calming it and helping it become stronger. Assure it of its security. Make it feel loved, talented, beautiful…everything you wanted to feel but didn't at that time. Tell your inner child that you love him/her. Shower into that letter all the love you wanted when you were a child. Don't hurry. Let the feelings flow through you before you pen them down. If you were abused in your childhood, write a second letter to the abuser *as an adult*. Use whatever choice words you want to and threaten to do whatever possible to bring that person to justice. Channel the fears of your child into anger as you write the letter. You are no longer weak; you are strong and can do what you want. Help your inner child face its fears and know that you've fought them. Your inner child has won…you are *free*.

Notes

Notes

Notes

Notes

Affirmations are like

seeds planted in soil.

Poor soil, poor growth. Rich soil,

ABUNDANT GROWTH.

The more you choose to think thoughts

that make you feel good, the

quicker the affirmations work.

~LOUISE L. HAY

Chapter 3

SELF-SUGGESTION MAGIC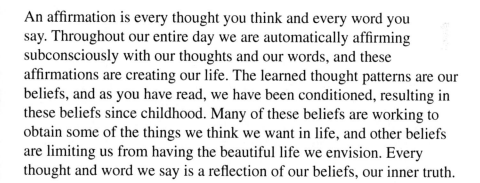

An affirmation is every thought you think and every word you say. Throughout our entire day we are automatically affirming subconsciously with our thoughts and our words, and these affirmations are creating our life. The learned thought patterns are our beliefs, and as you have read, we have been conditioned, resulting in these beliefs since childhood. Many of these beliefs are working to obtain some of the things we think we want in life, and other beliefs are limiting us from having the beautiful life we envision. Every thought and word we say is a reflection of our beliefs, our inner truth.

Our mental pattern is used by our subconscious. These learned patterns are the reason we automatically respond and react to the people and things in our life in the ways that we do. We need this to survive. We need to be able to react automatically to the happenings around us, which would be impossible if we had to take the time to determine every area of things every time some little thing was to happen. We have learned to respond quickly and efficiently with little effort. Problems show themselves when some of the foundational thought patterns we learned as a child were programmed through a trauma, dysfunction or some type of pain. There are no perfect parents, teachers or adults, therefore many children were taught patterns that would create their thoughts as an adult. And those thoughts have now created their life.

Positive Affirmations are typically short, positive statements. They are used to assist the subconscious by challenging the learned negative belief to change to a positive healthy belief. The construction of these statements is vital to their ability to work effectively.

Learning how to use positive affirmations is a very popular tool when it comes to personal development. Many amazing people you may know claim it is an essential part of their daily routine. Oprah Winfrey, Dr. Wayne Dyer, Louise Hay, Suze Orman, Jim Carrey and Will Smith are just a few.

The reason they use them is because they work.

Any self-discovery program or self-improvement workshop I have ever attended had some form of affirmation exercise incorporated as a key foundational tool for positive change. If you are ready to made a change and accept the changes that will take place in your life, the more productive affirmations will work for you.

When we choose to think and say positive affirmations, there are many times you may experience a strong negative feeling. This may happen because of your strength of your inner truth presumption. Your inner truth of your subconscious finds it easier to continue with its conditioned inner truth rather than challenging the new thoughts and words. Just as important as this awareness is the awareness when you experience a sense of peace and balance. You know your affirmations are working when you experience this emotion of joy.

To override your strong inner truth conditioning, repetitiveness of affirmations is the solution. As you continue, your thoughts will become much less resistant and your subconscious will be able to change your old patterns and beliefs with your own new, efficient, healthy and serviceable patterns and beliefs.

My experience with my own perceived inner truth in regards to body image and food was always very strong. Yet as I continually repeated my affirmations with conviction, I noticed I was becoming less resistant. I use affirmations even today in regards to these significant, crucial, personal conditioned behaviors. I am very gentle with myself when it comes to the programming and conditioning my subconscious has developed in these regards. I know, however, these affirmations are vital to my healing. I have a much better relationship with food than I have ever had in my entire life. My body size has transformed from a size 22 to a size 12 through the results of my dedication of my daily affirmation exercises. This transformation is my validation the affirmations are indeed working. I am also aware of those old behaviors and patterns when they sneak into my mind. This awareness allows me to understand and determine how strongly they are imbedded in my subconscious, as well as remind me to continue to do the exercises to reprogram my thought patterns. I also notice that when I have replaced my old beliefs with my own new positive belief patterns, good changes happen in many other aspects of my life as well as the belief pattern I had been working on directly.

Many people experience very effective changes immediately upon practicing affirmations, while others will feel very negative at first. Again, it really is about the individual's willingness to change, the desire to change, and the deep strength of the impact the dysfunctional behavior has conditioned upon the subconscious. Once a person does experience the benefits of affirmations, they learn a journey they will enjoy their entire life. Changes are inevitable as we grow, and when we obtain knowledge and develop skills to master our issues effectively, living a balanced life is inevitable. Affirmations make you feel better about yourself and your life. They have the ability to manifest positive change and remove those negative barriers so you can achieve the beautiful life you have always dreamed of.

Do you ever wonder why others don't use affirmations? Oh, they absolutely do! Did you know that nearly 90% of our thoughts are negative? Knowing this helps us all to understand why we struggle so often. These are called negative affirmations, and they can be more powerful than positive affirmations for the mere fact they seem easier to accept in the human mind. Do you understand why some people have a very difficult time changing their thoughts when they are not aware there is a choice to do so? When I learned of this, it assisted me greatly when I would witness the behaviors of others or recall behaviors of my past. Knowing this gave me even more desire to commit to choosing positive thoughts and words that are designed to challenge those negative beliefs and within time override them. It's all about awareness of thoughts, choosing to change them and making it a habit to reprogram the old, limited and dysfunctional patterns and beliefs.

To create affirmations for yourself, try to include words such as "I am" or "my" or any words that are to justify they are for you personally. When you include words such as this, they are very powerful to your subconscious brain. Your subconscious treats those words as a command to start working on what you say after you say them. Make certain you keep your affirmations in the present tense. The idea is you want your subconscious brain to see your goal as happening right now. If you speak your affirmation in the future tense, your subconscious mind will keep you always waiting for something to develop. An example of a properly phrased affirmation would be "I am full of energy and vitality at my ideal weight of 140." Remember to always keep your affirmations positive. You must state what you want. Your subconscious brain thinks in pictures, so do not ever think about what you do not want. For example, if you say you are no longer overweight, you most likely still get a picture in your mind of being overweight. For your affirmation to be effective, you would need to rephrase it as "I am fit and trim". It's also a good idea to keep your affirmations brief so you will be able to easily remember them.

I have created a list of affirmations for different areas of your life as examples to assist you in creating your own personal positive affirmations. Upon creating yours, perhaps you might want to write them down and place them in areas you will be certain to see them to remind yourself to say them. I have my personal affirmations framed next to my bed so I will see them every morning when I wake up and every evening before I go to sleep. I also have another framed affirmation at my office on my desk. Throughout my day, I read my affirmations and dedicate small portions of my day to reprogramming my subconscious mind.

AFFIRMATION *Examples*

Affirmations for Health

Every cell in my body vibrates with energy and health .

Loving myself heals my life. I nourish my mind, body and soul.

My body heals quickly and easily.

My body is healed, restored and filled with energy.

I have all the energy I need to accomplish
my goals and to fulfill my desires.

My body is a safe and pleasurable place for me to be.

I am healthy, happy and radiant.

I am healthy and full of energy and vitality.

I am perfectly healthy in body, mind and spirit.

God's love heals me and makes me whole.

My sleep is relaxed and refreshing.

I radiate good health.

All the cells of my body are daily submerged
in the perfection of my divine being.

I am well, I am whole, and I am strong and healthy.

My body is strong and filled with healing energy.

Affirmations for Joy and Happiness

My life is full of joy and delightful surprises.

My life is joy filled with love, fun and friendship.
All I need do is stop all criticism, forgive, relax and be open.

I choose love, joy and freedom, and I open my heart
and allow wonderful things to flow into my life.

My happiness is reflected in my smile and cheerful personality.

My pleasing and joyful personality is contagious.

I am always kind and helpful to strangers.

I spring out of bed with joy and excitement.

I am excited about the new day and look forward
to it with anticipation and interest.

I choose to be happy at the start of each day.

I laugh at myself with childish joy.

My sense of humor touches everyone around me.

My happiness continually brings me more happiness.

My happiness draws an abundant amount of blessings into my life.

Affirmations for Love

I know that I deserve Love and accept it now.

I give out Love, and it is returned to me multiplied.

I rejoice in the Love I encounter everyday.

I am filled with light, love and peace.

I treat myself with kindness and respect.

I give myself permission to shine.

I honor the best parts of myself and share them with others.

I am proud of all I have accomplished.

Today I give myself permission to be greater than my fears.

I am my own best friend and cheerleader.

I have many qualities, traits and talents that make me unique.

I am a valuable human being.

I love myself just the way I am.

I love and forgive myself for any past mistakes.

I look in the mirror and I love what I see.

Affirmations for Peace and Harmony

All my relationships are loving and harmonious.

I am at peace.

I trust in the process of life.

I am at peace with myself.

I am always in harmony with the Universe.

I am filled with the Love of God.

I am at peace with all those around me.

I have provided a harmonious place for myself and those I love.

The more honest I am with those around me,
the more love is returned to me.

I express anger in appropriate ways so that
peace and harmony are balanced at all times.

I am at one with the inner child in me.

I accept Peace and Harmony now.

My body is filled with balanced harmony.

I have peace in all areas of my life.

I exude peace and tranquility.

Affirmations for Prosperity

I prosper wherever I turn, and I know
that I deserve prosperity of all kinds.

The more grateful I am, the more reasons I find to be grateful.

I pay my bills with love as I know
abundance flows freely through me.

Prosperity flows to me and through my life.

I am blessed with overflowing abundance.

I am a child of God, worthy of abundant living.

I welcome my good.

I have a prosperous attitude that draws good to me.

I am open to new ideas and welcome an increase in income.

I am creating great wealth now.

I have an abundance of time to complete what I want to do.

I enjoy my abundance and share it freely with others.

I deserve to have financial abundance in my life now.

Affirmations for Self-Esteem

I believe in myself, and others do too.

I express my needs and feelings.

I am my own unique self—special, creative and wonderful.

I deserve to be happy and successful.

I have the power to change myself.

I can forgive and understand others and their motives.

I can make my own choices and decisions.

I am free to choose to live as I wish and to give priority to my desires.

I can choose happiness whenever I
wish no matter what my circumstances.

I am flexible and open to change in every aspect of my life.

I act with confidence, having a general plan,
and accept plans are open to alteration.

It is enough to have done my best.

I deserve to be loved.

I was created uniquely and for a purpose.

Affirmations for Weight Loss

I am the perfect weight for me.

I am fit and healthy.

I am losing weight right now.

I look and feel lighter.

I love the food that is good for my body.

I enjoy being healthy.

My body is strong.

I wear a smaller size.

I enjoy how I feel.

I am full of energy.

I am committed to my goals.

I effortlessly stay on track.

I choose to eat healthy food.

My body is the temple of my spirit.

I am thin and vibrant.

I look and feel amazing.

My body is beautiful.

I effortlessly take care of my body.

My body is an efficient machine.

I love how I look in this outfit.

Reflections FOR CHAPTER 4

Positive affirmations have a lot of positive energy. Simply repeating affirmations can have tremendous beneficial effects by themselves. However, doing certain affirmations in specific ways can increase their effectiveness many times over. Here are some affirmation techniques you could try doing to get the most out of positive affirmations:

Mirror talk: This technique is wonderful for improving your self image. Ideally, stand unclothed before a mirror and try to look for things that are good about your body. Try to find as many good things as you can and list them out loud, such as, "I like my neck" or "I like the way my hair curls around my face." Keep doing this till you convince yourself that you are perfect just the way you are!

Exercise talk: Do you exercise every day? No? It would be so beneficial for you! If you are one of those who exercise daily, it is a very effective time to repeat your affirmations. As you exercise, keep affirming, "I am strong," "I am thin," "I look good" or whatever it is that you are aiming for.

Write talk: Writing things down can do wonders in terms of healing and helping you emerge stronger. It can also help you with your positive affirmations. Write down your affirmations, ten times each. Mouth them as you write. Keep them somewhere you can see them everyday, and every once in a while stop and read them.

Dump talk: Write down your negative affirmations on a sheet of paper and throw them into a trash can. Whenever there's something you don't like doing, but have to do, write what you don't like about it and throw it away or burn it, indicating that you want to be done with the problem as soon as possible. Let your negative affirmations hold their talks with the trash dump!

Flame talk: Make one list of your positive affirmations and one for things you don't like about yourself, your life, your relationships… basically all your negative affirmations. Once done, get a candle and light it. As the flames leap up, burn your negative affirmation list. Watch as the flames lap it up and feel the negative thoughts release you from their hold.

Doing any of these techniques or repeating the affirmations given in the chapter might feel silly initially, but soon you'll grow used to it, and the results can be awesome! Regularity is the key. I have many positive affirmations and hardly any negative ones and still repeat my positive affirmations daily.

Notes

Notes

Notes

Notes

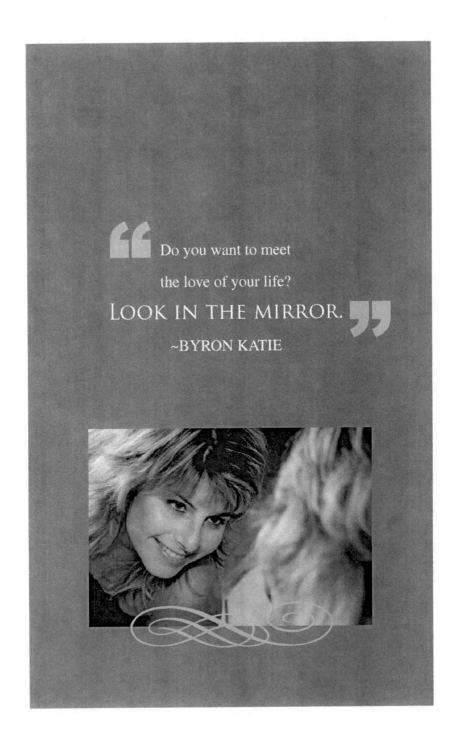

> " Do you want to meet
> the love of your life?
> LOOK IN THE MIRROR. "
> ~BYRON KATIE

Chapter 5

MIRROR, MIRROR ON THE WALL

Outside it was raining in Chicago. Looking out the large picture window to the direct right of our instructor, I saw that the rain was coming down in what looked like sheets of water. "Tears," I thought. "How appropriate." I was in a healing class and I had wept so much that day I felt like the weather was a metaphor for all the tears I had cried.

The instructor chimed in, "Now everyone pick up your mirror and look directly into your own eyes."

I picked up my mirror and looked directly into my own eyes for a moment, then immediately looked away. *"Oh my goodness,"* I gasped. *"Why is this so difficult?"* Upon looking around the class, I noticed it was difficult for many of the people. Some were clearly upset, some even angry. Many had tears running down their face, and some simply set the mirror back down on the table, stating they weren't able to do the exercise. I look in a mirror every day. I wash my face and brush my teeth. I spend quite a bit of time applying my makeup and doing my hair. Yet when I look in the mirror while preparing myself for others, I never "really" look in the mirror at "myself". The hours that I spend grooming is my "ego self"...the self I want everyone else to think that I am so they won't be able to see the "real self", the person that I *actually* am. I picked up the mirror again, and this time I was more gentle with myself. I looked compassionately into my own eyes, and the tears began to sting, then gently flow, warm salty liquid down each side of my face. Welcome to the real me.

Next the instructor told us to say our own name followed by,

"I love you and you are perfect just the way you are".

I heard others say the affirmation to themselves, yet I stayed silent and was simply amazed at what felt like meeting "me" for the first time in my life.

Go right now, look in the mirror into your own eyes, and say these words using your own name. *"Lisa, I love you and you are perfect just the way you are."* Go ahead, I will wait on you, and when you return we will discuss this exercise further.

How did you feel? Were you able to say those words to yourself? I remember when I actually said those words for the very first time, I didn't believe them. I simply just "said" them. Yet after some practice, I began to believe, I began to feel, I began to love myself and felt perfect just the way I was.

Mirror work is a very powerful tool. When we typically look into a mirror, most of us berate ourselves and say negative things to ourselves. I know I did this for as long as I could remember. Yet when you change this habit by looking into your own eyes and stating positive pronouncements, this is when you are able to begin gaining the positive effects.

Many people would argue that they simply do not have time to do all these exercises every day. Really? Every single morning I do my mirror work. I figure if I am going to be standing there brushing my teeth anyway, I might as well work on my emotional well being. Also, when I am driving to work and I am stopped in traffic, I look up into the rearview mirror and do a little healthy therapy then too. I'm going to be sitting there anyway, so why not?

The Advantages of Mirror Work:

~ Be confident in your abilities, strengths, competencies.

~ Become an optimist—see the possibilities for what they are, instead of seeing only the negative side of life.

~ Care for your inner child, spirit and soul.

~ Care for yourself to an extreme never experienced before.

~ Create an acceptance of yourself that no one else has ever given you.

~ Develop your own self-acceptance, confidence, self-worth, and love.

~ Discard your need for perfection, cast off your self-critical attitudes, and defeat idealization.

~ Enjoy life, relax, and have fun.

~ Identify the feelings you keep bottled up.

~ Learn the difference between the unhealthy way of being selfish or self-centered and the healthy option of being centered on self.

~ Make a pact with yourself to commit to recovering your self-esteem while living life to the fullest.

~ Praise yourself for your accomplishments, big and small.

~ Reconnect with the neglected parts of yourself.

~ Release your inner child by unleashing self-imposed restrictions.

~ Reward yourself for just being you.

~ Rid yourself of your habitual depression, negativity, and hostility towards yourself and your accomplishments.

~ Stop blaming yourself for mistakes and failures.

~ Stop the domino effect of self-destructiveness within your life.

~ Accept your body for what it is and understand the beauty and merit of your physical self.

~ Allow yourself to release those feelings in a healthy manner.

Positive outcomes of mirror work:

If you are conscientious about doing mirror work daily, you will begin to experience in 30 days:

~ increased body image

~ improved self-worth

~ acceptance

~ boost in self-confidence

~ view life in a more optimistic manner

~ become a leader of yourself—defend and protect
your rights and beliefs

~ positive mind chat

~ decreased need to hide behind "masks"
in order to hide your true self

~ increased sense of "well being"; positive sense of wellness

~ enhanced self-image

~ your ability to enjoy life in all its aspects

~ identify and relate to the feelings you experience in life,
instead of trying to block them

~ allow your inner child to become a part of yourself
in order to fully see the wonder of the world

~ lose the weight of the world on your spirit—lighten it up!

~ connect with those family and friends who you haven't
for fear of shame and unacceptance

~ share with others those parts of your life that you
have hidden in fear of judgement and embarrassment

~ accept your life for what it has been thus far, and
move on into what you want your life to become

If you ***do daily mirror work conscientiously***, you will begin to experience the following changes in your feelings:

<u>DECREASED</u>	~	<u>INCREASED</u>
defeated	~	triumphant
insecurity	~	self-assuredness
self-deprecating	~	self-reinforcing
heavy-hearted	~	lighthearted
unlikable	~	likable
revulsion	~	attraction
pessimism	~	optimism
discouraged	~	encouraged
shame	~	pride
goal-les	~	goal-oriented
loathing	~	appreciation
incompleteness	~	completeness
helplessness	~	competence
defectiveness	~	goodness
punishment	~	reward
reliance	~	independence
incapability	~	capability
unloved	~	self-loved
hatred	~	love
overwhelmed	~	in control
jealous	~	prideful
resentful	~	genial
tightfisted	~	generous
lacking	~	wholeness
valueless	~	valuable
worthlessness	~	value
despair	~	hope
pity	~	encouragement
impotence	~	strength
disgust	~	desire
loneliness	~	self-supported
unwanted	~	self-wanting
depressed	~	joyful

 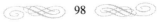

Typical Self-Affirmations Used in Mirror Work

Body Image Mirror Work

You look great !

You are stunning.

Everything about you is perfect the way it is.

You are special to me.

You are perfect.

Your body is an amazing miracle of nature.

Your body is handsome.

I love you and "your" body just the way we are.

Your body is beautiful.

I accept you just the way you are.

Your body is toned.

I love your stomach.

I love your body.

Your body is a wonderful creation.

You are gorgeous.

Your body is perfect.

I love every part of your beautiful body.

Increasing Visibility Mirror Work

You deserve to be surrounded by people who love,
support, and encourage you.

You deserve to be accepted the way you are.

You CAN remove your masks in order to show your true self.

You are a great person, and others deserve to get to know you.

Your ideas are important and deserve to be heard.

You have a wonderful personality that others deserve to enjoy.

You are special, and you will let others see how special you are.

You are a competent, capable person who deserves
to be seen and to have your rights respected.

There is nothing about you that needs to be hidden.

There is no need to hide anymore.

You deserve to be seen and heard.

You are an amazing, unique person who was
created for an important purpose.

You have an important contribution to make.

You are an intelligent person with wonderful talents
that are vital to assist your peers.

You are the star of an amazing production.

Inner Child Awareness Mirror Work

I respect your thoughts and feelings as much as I do my own.

I deserve to play as much as I work.

I deserve to act your age.

You are special to me.

You are my special friend.

I rely on you from now on.

I nurture you like you've never been nurtured before.

I listen and react more to your needs in the future.

I promise to no longer ignore you.

I love you.

I enjoy your company.

I deserve to play and to have fun.

I am here now to protect you.

I love spending time with you.

You are everything to me.

We enjoy many hours of laughter together.

I always take you seriously.

I always value you.

Mirror Work to Heal Feelings of Shame

You were made the way you were, and this is ok

Your thoughts and feelings are important and deserve to be shared.

You deserve to love and be loved in return.

I accept you as a whole, all parts of you together as one.

You have a great personality.

You did the best you could knowing what you did at the time.

You are a wonderful person.

There isn't anything that can keep you down.

Nothing can hold you back.

I love being you.

You deserve good things in life.

You are a beautiful person.

I accept you for who you are.

You are a spectacular person.

You keep getting better and better.

You can accomplish anything you choose to.

You are free to live your life.

I feel fortunate I was created to be you.

Post Weight Loss Mirror Work

You are toned.

You are beautiful.

You are an athlete.

You are thin.

You are healthy.

Your body is the right size for me.

You exercise each day to retain my health.

You eat what my body needs to survive without self-punishing.

You can still enjoy your favorite foods without feeling guilty.

I am so proud of you.

You are at the right weight for me.

You enjoy eating healthy cuisine.

Staying fit is easy for you.

You are the essence of good health.

Your weight is healthy.

You have boundless energy.

You are flexible and free.

Your body is vibrant and light.

You enjoy eating fruits and vegetables.

Self-Acceptance Mirror Work

I accept myself just the way you are.

I accept that you are human.

I accept that you are not perfect.

I accept that you are responsible for my own life.

I accept that you can choose to focus your attention on yourself first
so that you can be "real and authentic" to others.

I accept that you have self-defeating behaviors
you can choose to change.

I accept that changing your behaviors will take some time.

I accept the way you were created.

I accept there are some circumstances beyond your control.

I accept your personality.

I accept your natural talents and abilities you were blessed with.

I accept your body as it was created.

I accept success as it comes to you.

I accept you were created for a purpose.

I accept you are a unique being.

I accept you have complete authority over me.

I accept it will take you some effort and time to change.

Self-Encouragement Mirror Work

You've done such a good job, keep up the great work!

You are the best at being you.

You are brilliant!

You are amazing!

You love yourself as you love your neighbor.

You've come a long way, baby!

You are special to me!

You are my best friend.

Together we make quite a team, a real dynamic duo.

Nice going. I knew you could do it!

I'm so proud of you!

I really can rely on you. Thanks!

You are SO talented!

You are so smart!

Excellent work!

I'm so fortunate to have you as a friend!

You are the best!

You make me so happy!

You are great company.

Together we can do anything!

I'm never bored when I'm with you.

You make me smile.

Self-Forgiveness Mirror Work

You can do nothing that can't be forgiven.

You deserve to be forgiven.

You are worthy of being forgiven.

You are not perfect, and failures or mistakes are inevitable.

You are a loving, caring person.

You and I are best friends.

There is no need for you to be so hard on yourself.

I forgive you for ignoring me for so long.

I forgive you for being human.

It is okay, I love you.

I forgive you, you did the best you could with what you knew.

You deserve to "let it go".

You no longer need to feel bad.

I love you under all circumstances.

You are going to be okay.

You are a wonderful, sensitive human being.

You have a compassionate heart.

I am quick to forgive you.

I see in your eyes that you are hurting; I am here for you.

I love you.

Reflections FOR CHAPTER 5

Now, this might come as a surprise to some of you, but it is the truth: many of us perceive ourselves very differently than others do. What we see in the mirror is often a distorted image of ourselves. For some, this distortion is more so than for others. What do I mean by that? For example, people with eating disorders like anorexia and bulimia perceive themselves as fat when they stand before a mirror, but to others they might look sickly thin.

In their case, the perceived distortion is extreme, but it does exist to some extent in the rest of us, too. We see things our mind makes us think are there. So, for instance, even though you have a pretty nose, you might be unaware of it because you think your nose is flat and that is what you perceive when you look in the mirror. And, if someone were to compliment you on the fine shape of your nose, you would be taken aback.

So, how can you make your mirror speak to you in a manner that is real, in a language that speaks the truth? How can you look in the mirror and see yourself as you are and love the image that stares back at you?

1. Clear your mind of its misconceptions. Remember your mind can be a liar. It does not always tell the truth. Discard all the negative affirmations your mind brings forth when you stand before a mirror. "Oh my God! That scar looks so terrible. My face looks awful." Stop right there! Discard that negative thought and bring in positive ones. "The scar isn't really noticeable and it makes me unique. I am pretty."

2. Have a good friend, one who can give you an honest and uncritical review of all your perceived faults. "Is my forehead too small?" "Do I look fat?" "Have I increased around the waist?" "What do you think of this scar ? Does it look too bad?" Try not to wear her out, but if you are having a hard time convincing your mind of its ill-perceived mirror images, someone else's positive affirmation can help drive it home.

Think of all the negativity that crosses your mind each day when you stand before the mirror. Make a promise to yourself to do your best to get rid of those thoughts. Your self-image is in your hands. Bridge the gap between the eye and your mind. See what you want to see and not what your mind tells you to. Face the world feeling more beautiful, more confident...the world's your stage!

Notes

Notes

Notes

Notes

" As human beings, our GREATNESS lies not so much in being able to remake the world—that is the myth of the 'atomic age'— as in being able to remake ourselves. "

~GANDHI

Chapter 6

SUBCONSCIOUS REPROGRAMMING— OPTIMIZING YOUR MIND

I recall a conversation I had with a couple of former classmates of mine at a high school class reunion. I was on the planning committee, and it was the night of the big event. All of the attendees were mingling, eating, reminiscing about yesteryear when one of them at the table I was sitting at began to complain about the music genre. Months of preparation, time and money with the aim to try to please everyone was discussed many times with the group during those planning committee meetings. Needless to say, I was well into my transformation enough to know this was most likely not going to be accomplished. We are all different and we all have our unique likes and dislikes, those things we prefer and those things we do not.

Once the gentleman complained again, I explained to him in front of everyone in a gentle voice, "I understand you. Please understand it is almost impossible to please everyone at the same time, especially in a group this size. What would you like to hear, and I will see if I am able help you."

The woman I was sitting next to leaned into me, looked me in the eyes and said, "Lisa, what happened to you!?"

The reason I am writing about this particular event is because those who watched me grow knew how I would have responded before I was on a healing journey. Years prior to this, I would have reacted with emotions of anger and actions of ego and then calmed down with a "people pleaser" mentality. Before my healing journey, my emotions and actions were a mess, and of course when I would act out negatively it would begin attracting more negative situations and people into my life. I was on a vicious, never stopping merry-go-round of negative vibrations.

Standing at the bar, waiting for a glass of wine, another classmate of mine, Darren Tuggle, and I began chatting.

"Lisa, you are really an awesome person, why didn't we hang out more in school?" he asked.

I laughed and said, "Well, because I wasn't really awesome when we were *in* school."

This guy was an awesome human being who everyone really liked in high school. He had a good energy about him back then, and he carried that same energy with him through the years to that night at the class reunion. He seemed to always attract good things to himself. Before my healing, I would have thought he was just one of the lucky ones. I know otherwise now. I know he worked on developing his inner programming.

Those who would meet me for the first time today would have a very difficult time believing I was such a pessimist, being that today I am extremely outgoing. I've been told I produce a positive liveliness within others, yet before my journey everywhere I looked I found the negativity in the situation, the place, the object, the person as well as the reflection in the mirror. Life sucked. Life was crap. Life wasn't fair. I didn't trust others and was certain everyone would hurt me or leave me if I got too close. And since I thought those thoughts, you know what happened? Yep, my life sucked. My life was crap. My life wasn't fair, and everyone allowed to get close to me betrayed me then left me. I created my own negative life with my negative subconscious programming.

When I began learning about subconscious programming, I read that many scientific studies have proven that pessimism is a life-threatening disease. In addition to interfering with our own immune system, it can also have a destructive and damaging effect on every aspect of our lives: our relationships with others, our career, and our capacity to grow and succeed as an individual. I was a prime example of this statement. My immune system was most certainly affected with illnesses as well as the disease of depression and obesity. I always seemed to be in some kind of drama in my relationships. By the time I had reached 28 years old, I had been married three times. My life was a prime example of the effects of being a pessimist.

SUBCONSCIOUS MIND

Consciousness is a thin aspect of our mind. On the other hand, the subconscious mind is a vast storehouse of memories and associations, and the driver of a great deal of human behavior. Think of a basketball and a baseball...the baseball represents your conscious mind, and the basketball, your unconscious mind.

Most people try to use the relatively weak (by comparison) ability of their conscious mind, when simply bringing their unconscious resources onboard would allow them to accomplish things and make changes with relative ease.

BELIEF SYSTEMS AND THE SUBCONSCIOUS

Ask someone, "what do you believe about doorknobs?" and they will likely look at you as though you were crazy.

Yet, one thing we can know beyond the shadow of a doubt is that everyone who walks up to a door, grabs the doorknob, turns it, and opens the door has an unconscious belief that when doorknobs are turned, doors are likely to open.

Approximately 90% of human behavior is automated

Approximately 90% of human behavior is automated, meaning that we do not engage in conscious thoughts or make conscious decisions about much of what we do. When we sit down, we have faith-based on a belief about chairs-that the chair will support our weight...even if it is a chair we have never seen before.

Imagine how overwhelming life would be if we had to think about every doorknob, or every chair, before we turned them or sat down in them.

Clearly, doorknobs and chairs seem rather innocuous, but remember, each person has unconscious beliefs about relationships, food, work, health, money...you name it.

This is where things can get tricky. If someone believes that relationships always have a sad ending, can you see where, over time, they may develop a secondary belief that says, "It's not worth getting into relationships...it's just too darn painful!"?

Let me ask you a few questions. ***What do you believe about:***

~ Love
~ Money
~ Friendship
~ Career
~ Happiness
~ Health
~ Children
~ Community Service

Chances are very good that at least on several of the areas listed—if not all—you had a pause…a blank…where you really came up with very little.

Now, if you are over the age of 15, you almost certainly have fairly strong beliefs about each of these areas. Yet, because your answers to "what do you believe about…?" didn't just come tumbling out immediately, you can also be sure that your beliefs, at least up until now, have been operating well below your conscious awareness.

The part of this that most people don't get—partly because of an abundance of misinformation—is that your subconscious or unconscious mind is not "buried" under all kinds of mystical layers that require years of psychotherapy to reveal and/or work with.

See, as you've been reading this, you've likely been unaware of the sensations in the third toe on your right foot…the temperature of the second knuckle on the first finger of your left hand…the feeling of air moving past your nostrils as you breathe…the memory of your last birthday, or that particular day with your best friend when you were a child, the one that really means a lot to you. In fact, there are literally millions of things you are not aware of…that is, until your attention is taken to them, and then…boom…there they are.

Imagine walking into a pitch black room. You have a flashlight, but it is not yet turned on. Suddenly, you turn it on and shine it at the wall in front of you; anything you shine it on comes into view and captures your attention. Interestingly, anything you are not shining your light on is, for the most part, nonexistent as far as your awareness is concerned.

As you change walls, the wall that you had just been shining your light on lingers momentarily in your awareness, even as new items come into view. But with time, the memory of the first wall fades. And so it goes with the "flashlight" of our day-to-day attention. Our unconscious is anything we are unaware of or are not focused on at any given moment. However, in the blink of an eye, we can shift our attention to other things.

In short, for everything new that we bring into our awareness, we are simultaneously shifting other things outside of our awareness.

Those who are masters of their emotions and states of mind are also masters of their attention, and thus, their subconscious or unconscious mind.

How would *you* like to become the master of your attention?

Here are some exercises you can do to rapidly expand your awareness and aid you in being able to shift from one aspect of your experience to another at will.

Exercise #1:

Go for a walk someplace different each time, and place your attention on the sounds in your environment. Each time your attention is pulled away to something else, keep bringing it back to the sounds. Pay attention not only to the external sounds, but to the sounds inside your mind, as well as things you are saying to yourself, for this is as much a part of your environment as anything on the outside.

Exercise #2:

Go for a walk someplace different each time, and place your attention on the smells in your environment. Each time your attention is pulled away to something else, keep bringing it back to the smells. Pay attention not only to the external smells, but to the smells inside your mind, as well as smells contained in and associated with memories, for this is as much a part of your environment as anything on the outside.

Exercise #3:

Go for a walk someplace different each time, and place your attention on the things that are red in your environment (make it a different color each time). Each time your attention is pulled away to something else, keep bringing it back to the things that are red. Pay attention not only to the external red, but to the red inside your mind, and red that is contained in and associated with memories as well, as this is as much a part of your environment as anything on the outside.

Exercise #4:

Go for a walk someplace different each time, and place your attention on the feelings and sensations of things in your environment. Each time your attention is pulled away to something else, keep bringing it back to the feelings and sensations. Pay attention not only to the external sensations, but to the sensations inside your mind, as well as feelings that are contained in and associated with memories, for this is as much a part of your environment as anything on the outside.

Exercise #5:

Turn the volume off on your television and watch a talk show, one where people are having a debate of some kind. Notice how much more you become aware of things like facial expressions, gestures and posture when you can't incorporate voices.

Exercise #6:

Put on your favorite movie and wear a blindfold so you are forced to only listen to the movie. Notice how many nuances of what is being said are present that you never noticed before.

Exercise #7:

Ask a friend to hold your hand and take you for a walk outside. Notice how much your awareness of your balance and the sensation of your shifting weight become heightened with the absence of sight.

As you complete these exercises each time, you'll find that your ability to shift your attention grows by leaps and bounds. This will lead to an increase of confidence.

To remind yourself of how vast your unconscious capacity truly is, ask yourself, "What am I *not* aware of right now?" The answer, of course, is "almost everything!"

When you are sad, what are you *not* aware of at that moment?

When you are angry, what are you *not* aware of at that moment?

Anytime we are feeling less than happy, our attention is on something. But that something represents such a tiny fraction of things it *could* be on, things that if our attention was shifted to, the sadness or other negative feeling would immediately begin to dissipate.

I invite you to set out to become the director of your experience by directing your attention. Think of it...Stephen Spielberg is a master at knowing exactly where to focus the attention of the cameras in each scene in order to move the emotions of the movie fans. You, too, can begin moving your own emotions by deciding where your attention will linger, and more importantly, where it won't.

Reflections
FOR CHAPTER 6

Years of subconscious programming are very difficult to reprogram. For some who have had a traumatic experience which they harbor in their subconscious, asking them to forget it is like asking them to forget their name. It is very difficult. Some people might unconsciously close up on certain things because they have had bad experiences regarding those things in the past.

You must have noticed how some people refuse to open up and let others see their emotions because they've been emotionally hurt before. That person may not realize it, but in all their actions you can see their emotional detachment. It's their subconscious trying to protect them from a repeat of the same incident. And because of that, they end up missing so much that life has to offer in terms of love, joy and happiness.

Today, sit down and try to think of all your past experiences, good and bad, that you think have molded the person you are today. Think of all the qualities you have, again good and bad, and try and pinpoint where they stem from. Think! Think of what memory, what experience in your past contributed to your actions today. Maybe you had a bad business deal in the past and have refused to trust people since then. Try and zone in on the reason.

Once you've identified the cause for the negative parts of you, of the person you are, analyze if that quality, that behavior is warranted. One person unworthy of your trust does not make everyone else the same. If you feel you'd be better off without a certain emotion, have a heart to heart with your subconscious. Tell it that you don't want that experience affecting your life anymore and want to replace it with a more positive outlook. Positive affirmations are a great tool in subconscious reprogramming.

It is much easier to program than reprogram your subconscious. Here are some small mental exercises you can undertake to program your subconscious to expect good and work towards it:

1. Fast Forward To The Future:
You probably have goals in your life. Imagine you've achieved your goals and walk, talk and behave as if you've tasted the success. Your subconscious will pick up on those feelings and help you become more receptive to things that can contribute to that success.

2. Question Yourself:
Don't simply wish for things, question how you can achieve them. Your subconscious is more attuned to respond to plans than wishes.

Your subconscious defines who you are; program it so you can be who you want to be.

> *Dear God, Please send to me the*
> ## SPIRIT OF YOUR PEACE.
> *Then send, dear Lord, the spirit of peace from me to all the world. Amen.*

~MARIANNE WILLIAMSON

Notes

Notes

Notes

Notes

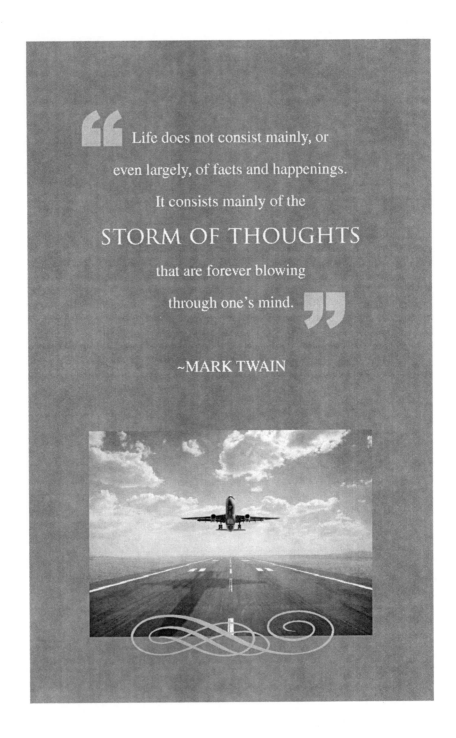

"Life does not consist mainly, or even largely, of facts and happenings. It consists mainly of the

STORM OF THOUGHTS

that are forever blowing through one's mind.

~MARK TWAIN

Chapter 7

INTRODUCING ...
YOUR ADRENAL GLANDS

WHAT IS THE
"FIGHT OR FLIGHT RESPONSE?"

This primary physiologic response establishes the basis of modern day stress medicine. The "fight or flight response" is our body's original and natural response that prepares the body to "run away from" or "fight" anything we believe would hurt us or threaten our life. Do you know what excessive stress does to our bodies? When under large amounts of stress—sourced internally or externally—a "knee-jerk" reaction is triggered within our body, known as the "fight or flight" response. This trigger is ingrained within our genetic design and represents the inherited wisdom used to protect ourselves. This response correlates directly to the hypothalamus, a part of the brain that controls a variety of functions, including hunger, fatigue, and thirst. When stimulated, the hypothalamus activates a process of chemical and nervous releases that prepares our body for action. When our fight or flight response has been triggered, our body releases hormones such as adrenaline, noradrenaline, and cortisol into our bloodstream, forcing extreme bodily changes. Breathing becomes faster and shallower, increasing oxygen in the bloodstream. Heart rate quickens, while blood vessels and airways become dilated. Blood is directed away from digestive functions and towards muscles in order to provide energy if quick action is needed. Pupils are also dilated in order to receive more signals to the optic nerve, sharpening our eyesight. Pain receptors are blocked by adrenaline, allowing our bodies to ignore pain until the threat has passed. We become more impulsive, acting on base instinct rather than taking excess time to think things through. Even our immune system activates in preparation for injury. Unconsciously our bodies provide the physical and mental tools necessary for whichever action we take: fight or flight. Our bodies become highly alert, scanning and examining our environment for the apparent threat.

When our bodies have become primed for fight or flight, we see everything around us as a possible threat to our survival.

Because the fight or flight response is one of our more basic functions, we ignore our rational self—the side of ourselves that tries to talk us out of impulse actions—in favor of a more impulsive, offensive being. Like airport security during a terrorist threat, we operate in a highly alert state. We can easily overreact to offhand comments. Fear is magnified. We act in a paranoid fashion. In fact, the very root meaning of paranoid is to guard against worry. Our minds perceive everything as potential threats. Our center of attention is restricted to those threats. Instead of seeing things clearly, we filter them through fear-tinted glasses.

When stuck in "fight or flight" mode, we are unable to see things clearly. It is unfeasible to see things positively, or even just have an open mind. Our body doesn't allow us the resources to think of anything but our own survival. When focused on fear, how can we even conceive the thought of love? Rationalizing our choices and acknowledging the consequences is impossible. Long term results of our choices aren't included within our field of mental vision. We are focused on short-term survival, not the long-term consequences of our beliefs and choices. When overwhelmed, we tend to focus on different sources of stress one at a time, instead of looking at the larger picture, creating a multitude of small crisis . By doing this, we are unable to stay calm and enjoy life. When our life is centered around a crisis, we tend to feel all our time is needed to solve the problem, with no reprieve in sight. Mental and physical exhaustion is unavoidable. This exhaustion is what motivates us to change ourselves for the better. We are forced to examine the bigger picture of our lives—our beliefs, values and goals are open for our inspection.

The fight or flight response protects us from predators—for our ancestors, wolves and aggressive, hungry tigers were primary threats. Because this response is designed to act for the sole purpose of our survival, there is no greater weapon, offensively or defensively. As part of the response, hormones, adrenalin included, flood through the body, increasing and focusing on bodily functions. These hormones are the cause of superhuman abilities: people lifting cars off of victims, ripping doors off their hinges, and running faster than usually possible. Adrenaline allows us to ignore the side of us that would rationalize our abilities and tell ourselves that "we can't do that" in times when we are forced to protect and defend ourselves and our beliefs.

What are the modern day predators, and what danger do they pose? When faced with physical danger, the fight or flight response is priceless. Fortunately, modern day predators consist more of daily activities—late payment on bills, construction on the interstate when we're already running late, having our credit card denied, the threat of being fired, or the possibility of losing a valuable relationship with our spouse or with a friend. No matter how intangible or menial the threat, our fight or flight response is activated, just like when the doctor lightly taps our knee to elicit the "knee jerk" reaction. These stress hormones saturate our bodies multiple times daily for occurrences that have no effect on our physical survival.

When faced with physical danger, the fight or flight response is priceless.

Once activated, what is the physical conclusion of Fight or Flight? In accordance with its name, the fight or flight response demands some kind of physical exertion in order to return stress hormones back to their normal level. Once the perceived threat is no longer present, due to either our dominance over it or having fled from it, we return to a state of normalcy.

Does the fight or flight response still work with today's predators? With modern day predators, we don't always have the option of flight or fight, even though we are subconsciously telling our body that we must be prepared for those options. Unfortunately, a lot of today's problems require patience and control, neither of which is easily done with that much adrenaline in our system. Rush hour traffic, an argument with our boss, or a denied credit card activates the full onrush of adrenaline, but doesn't allow a physical release. This causes us to be irrational, aggressive, hyper-alert, and over-reactive. These behaviors can actually act against our survival instinct, causing behaviors such as road rage or fighting with your boss or the waiter. Other ineffective responses would be to dine and dash, or walking out during a discussion.

Are there negative effects from over-activation of our fight or flight response? Adrenalin is designed to be used up directly after its original surge: fight or flight. Because much of our modern day stress is mental, adrenaline stays in the system, instead of returning to its normal levels. Short-term negative effects include headache, indigestion, fatigue, and depression. Negative long-term effects on the body, especially when too much of it is in the system too frequently, include higher blood pressure and heart rate, infertility, faster aging process, allergies, susceptibility to infection and arthritis.

In order to protect ourselves from our modern day mental predators, we must be aware of the signals of fight or flight. These can present themselves as muscle tension, stomach "butterflies", racing heart, headache or change in breathing, whether it be faster or deeper. Other symptoms include anxiety, nervousness, depleted concentration, depression, frustration, anger, unexplained sadness or fear.

Stress does not always present itself as what we recognize as stress.

It can often only be recognized by what physical symptoms we express, including teeth grinding, soreness in joints, and loss of hair. In other examples, we may also show stress emotionally, such as being consistently upset, angry, or sad, without having a specific source to pin that emotion on.

When we acknowledge that we are in the fight or flight response, we are able to start the process to cope with our stress. Sometimes having the hyper-abilities of fight or flight can be beneficial—being decisive and focused on a problem helps to solve it. In other times, having tunnel vision on a problem might cause it to take longer to solve. For example, focusing on one number at a time in a Sudoku puzzle may make it impossible to solve. But by seizing on any available opportunities to fill an empty box with a number, and looking at the bigger picture, the puzzle becomes considerably less complicated. When we familiarize ourselves with the physical and mental symptoms of fight or flight, we can avoid overreacting to non-life-threatening events or fears. We can pick and choose which effects of fight or flight we wish to use to make the most of every stressful situation.

The fight or flight response is a genetically ingrained alarm system—it alerts us to external (and sometimes internal) threats. Our system is extremely sensitive, responding to any level of danger, even those we may not consciously recognize. Failure to activate this alarm system means one thing to our bodies: death. Understanding this provides us with two stress reduction tools.

One tool is changing our environment. Any action we take that makes us feel safer helps remove stress. This includes walking on the other side of the street from a suspicious looking character, walking in groups at night, and avoiding places that make you feel uncomfortable. Some of these things we do unconsciously—how often do we walk into a burning building? Other actions include spending time with people who support and care for us, avoiding abusive relationships, and taking jobs that allow us to grow in our careers. We can also choose to live our lives with purpose, allowing ourselves to believe in a grander scheme of things other than daily menial duties and believing in a power greater than ourselves such as God, the Universe, the Inner Source, the Holy Spirit, etc.

The second stress reduction tool is altering our perceptions. This shift of thinking goes along with the "glass half full" cliché. We must allow ourselves the opportunity to change our thinking, attitudes, perspectives, and reactions that we have to events. Another wonderful cliché for this alteration is "when life gives you lemons, make lemonade." We don't actually throw away the lemons; we use the parts of them that we want and add something enjoyable (sugar) to it, with a beneficial result.

Physical exercise allows our bodies to metabolize excess resource

Physical exercise allows our bodies to metabolize excess resources —extra energy, extra nutrients, extra hormones, especially stress hormones. As we exercise, we restore our body to a more natural, balanced state, allowing our mind to calm. Exercise also gives us endorphins, a hormone produced by the hypothalamus and known for its effects of pain relief and feelings of well being. When we feel better, we tend to focus on the positive aspects of our lives, and we are more open to others' beliefs and values.

When exercising to stay in shape, medical examiners encourage a 30 minute workout with a consistent raised heartbeat. Stress reducing workouts are a bit easier—working out to the level of breaking a sweat for five minutes will allow the body to use up excess stress hormones. Jogging up and down stairs, jumping jacks, jogging down the street and back, sit ups, pushups, etc. for five minutes allows the body to achieve internal balance. Many of these activities can be done anywhere, in your home or office, refreshing us for the rest of the day.

What is mind chatter?

"My God, I am so stupid!"

"He probably won't call because I'm not worth being a priority to anyone."

"I'll never finish this."

"She only likes me because I do things for her."

"I look like a big cow in this dress."

"Oh great, another red light."

"I am a terrible mom."

"Mom likes him better."

"Dad is so disappointed in me."

"I never do anything right."

"They will probably be late."

"I don't trust that person."

"Today is going to suck."

"Why did I say that?"

"I am so fat."

"I wonder how bad I would feel if _____ happened?"

"I don't matter."

"It's all my fault."

"I should be ashamed."

"Why would anyone want to be with me?"

"What did I do to deserve this?"

This is an example of approximately fifteen minutes of the mind chatter that would be automatically running through my mind before my healing journey. Mind Chatter is the continuous flow of thoughts and rationalities that is consistently streaming through our minds, which the majority of the time is negative and self-insulting. Survival requires constant awareness of internal and external threats, real or imaginary. Constant alertness is one of the major activations for fight or flight, and it requires the most resources that exhaust us, body and mind.

Once we mute the mind chatter
and calm the fight or flight response,
we find an inner sanctuary within our mind.

This place gives us the freedom to bypass our fears and anxieties and find an understanding of truth and love. Spending time within this inner sanctuary calms our physical body, shutting down our counterproductive survival instincts and cleaning our body of negative physiological and biochemical changes.

One of the best ways to find the way to our inner sanctuaries is the relaxation response. The relaxation response, similar to the fight or flight response, is a "knee jerk" reaction. It will work, and there are multiple ways to activate it. It is the antidote to the fight or flight response. The relaxation response stimulates the hypothalamus, the very part of the brain that provides our stress hormones, to send out the chemical cure that neutralizes the hyper-alert function of the fight or flight response.

Benefits of the relaxation response include: decreased respiration, blood pressure, pulse, and oxygen levels in the body. This can also improve our sense of well being mentally, physically, and spiritually.

It is very important to take the time to exercise our relaxation response "muscle". When our bodies are tired, the best solution is to allow them to rest. The same goes for the fight or flight response—we must allow our bodies rest from this state of being. To do this, we must exercise the relaxation response in order to reap the beneficial chemical, mental, and physical effects. However, while some people feel the immediate effects of the relaxation response, others don't, just as some people can feel refreshed with a twenty minute nap while others need more time. We know that the sleep is good for us; we just may not feel the effects of it right away. Feeling good is an added benefit. Of course, practice, practice, practice is important in order to gain the benefits of the response.

There are many ways to prompt the physiological benefits of the relaxation response. The easiest is with a simple two-step method as follows:

1. Focus on a positive, meaningful mantra. Some people find uplifting Bible verses effective, as well as short prayers, while others prefer words such as unity, hope, faith and love.

2. It is inevitable that your mind, unused to such inner tranquility, will wander back towards the instinctive mind chatter. When this happens, simply refocus your thoughts on your mantra. Allow these thoughts to pass through yourself, paying them as little attention as possible. Intrusive thoughts are our mind's way of blocking our ability to heal. ("This is silly, why am I bothering? I have better things to do." "It's not working, therefore I should just give up now!" "I hope no one sees me." Tonight I must go to the grocery store because I'm out of milk again!" etc.) Just the attempt of practicing the relaxation response, however well it is done, will

deliver the beneficial effects to our bodies. As with anything worth doing, practice makes perfect, and daily sessions will be highly beneficial. Ten minutes once or twice a day will provide maximum results, even if they aren't measurable in the usual sense. It is helpful to our bodies, similar to taking a daily vitamin. The inner tranquility we find without mind chatter and hyper vigilance is freeing, allowing us to be aware and conscious of attitudes, events, beliefs, and ideas that have no threat to ourselves.

There are other ways to quiet the mind. The relaxation response is a physical response (like our heart rate or respiratory rate), and there are many additional ways to activate it. They include:

~ Stating over and over quietly or aloud a chosen word such as "Love" or "Calm"

~ Speaking repetitive prayers or scriptures you feel are calming

~ Taking very deep, slow breaths while focusing on each breath

~ Concentrate on each muscle in your body, starting from your head to your toes, while tightening them and then relaxing them

~ Practice an exercise such as Pilates, tai chi or yoga

A method of meditation called "mindfulness meditation" that, instead of ignoring the world around us, opens our awareness to the smallest of actions and reactions, will also elicit the relaxation response. For example, when going for a walk, one might comment on the birds in the trees, the leaves falling, the touch and smell of grass, or the colors of flowers. Also comment upon the physical reactions of the body, including sweating, goose bumps, movement of the legs and arms, are the hands clenched or loose, is hunger or thirst present? By saying aloud all of these characteristics of ourselves and our environment, we have opened ourselves to the world as a whole, instead of just identifying the threatening aspects of it.

The point to this activity is to simply perceive our environment and ourselves without making any judgments about it—this is akin to letting go of the disruptive thoughts of inactive meditation. Emotional mindfulness is also a part of active meditation...commenting on our feelings and the source of these feelings without attaching any negative or positive connotations to them. The key is to simply notice our world and our feelings. An example would be: "I am feeling hurt. Tears are streaming down my face. I am remembering how sad I was the day that happened. I am becoming tense right now. I am feeling hurt again." Recognition and acknowledgement of the feelings and the source of them is the primary goal.

Other simple ways to quiet the mind may be walking along the beach and listening to the sounds of the water. Or perhaps walking through a forest or park to listen to the trees, crickets, or birds. Sometimes I enjoy a warm bath or sitting in a favorite chair listening to the sounds of nature. These easy and stress free activities can be immensely beneficial to finding our inner peace.

WE DON'T LEARN TO SWIM IN THE OCEAN.

When we were little, we were taught to swim in about a foot of water, increasing the depth as we became more proficient with the activity. Why should practicing inner peace be any different? We need to practice quiet moments in times of little to no danger—that is, moments that are already quiet. Right before bed is the perfect opportunity. In order to quiet our minds, we need to be aware of our thoughts and feelings in order to set them aside. Being patient is a large part of quietness, one that many of us are not very good at. But with practice, calming our minds will become automatic.

My hope is you have learned from this chapter that in order to have the freedom to pick and choose those attitudes and beliefs that are beneficial to our well being, calming the mind and body is necessary.

The most effective way to do this is to disregard mind chatter by activating the relaxation response, our very own antidote to the fight or flight response. This allows us to find the tranquility within our mind in order to heal ourselves and open up to new perceptions, beliefs, and ideas that may be beneficial to the rest of our lives. When we do so, we might find that our mind is like a pond of water... restless thoughts are like trash cluttering the surface, not allowing us to see through the pool. But when we remove the trash and allow new perceptions to grow like water lilies, we find that our mind, like the pool, is a beautiful thing indeed.

Reflections FOR CHAPTER 7

I am not going to ask you to avoid the flight or fight response. It is as natural as breathing and has considerable survival value. The problem starts when it becomes a constant fixture in your life. The problem with our current world, with most of the predators we face today, is that you can neither fight them nor take flight. For instance, most of the stress that we face each day can't be fought against, nor can you run away from it. You've just got to face it.

In such difficult scenarios, the trick is to channel some of the adrenaline out of your system to calm yourself to ensure that you can face the problem with a logical mind and not when your brain is still forcing you to choose between fight and flight and you are considerably overwhelmed.

As I've mentioned before, physical exercises are the most potent way of expending the extra adrenaline flowing in your blood. Breathing exercises are excellent for getting your calm and clear-headedness back. Here's one simple breathing exercise called the Three Part Breath. But before you start doing it, it helps to relieve some of the muscular tension by moving your limbs, neck and if possible, taking a short walk.

Three-Part Breath

Choose a quiet place which offers little or ideally no distractions.

You could sit straight on a chair with feet planted firmly on the floor or lie down on the floor with your spine straight. Choose the one you'd feel comfortable in.

1. Inhale and expand your abdomen. Let it inflate. Then let your breath move to your rib cage and slowly to your upper chest.

2. Exhale in the reverse direction by breathing out from your upper chest, then expelling the air in your rib cage and eventually your abdomen. Feel your abdominal muscles contract as the breath moves out.

3. Some people find placing their hands on their chest and abdomen is helpful in directing their breath.

A minute of the *Three Part Breath* initially can be extended to five minutes with practice.

Sometimes, you can avoid the daily stresses by carrying out small changes in your lifestyle. For instance, not taking on more work than you could possibly do will ensure that you aren't struggling to meet deadlines. See what little tweaks you can do in your life to keep the fight or flight response at bay.

Notes

Notes

Notes

Notes

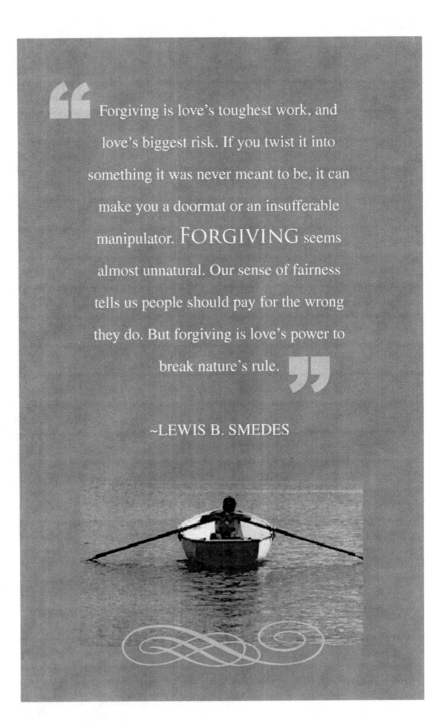

> Forgiving is love's toughest work, and love's biggest risk. If you twist it into something it was never meant to be, it can make you a doormat or an insufferable manipulator. FORGIVING seems almost unnatural. Our sense of fairness tells us people should pay for the wrong they do. But forgiving is love's power to break nature's rule.

~LEWIS B. SMEDES

Chapter 8

FORGIVING IS SOMETHING YOU <u>DO</u> FOR YOU

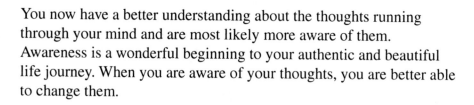

You now have a better understanding about the thoughts running through your mind and are most likely more aware of them. Awareness is a wonderful beginning to your authentic and beautiful life journey. When you are aware of your thoughts, you are better able to change them.

A few years back, I was speaking with a psychologist regarding negative thoughts, spinning thought processes and their relation to anxiety. He told me one of the struggles some of his clients experienced was when they learned to be aware of *when* they were having a negative thought, but they had a difficult time automatically being able to change it to a positive thought. So, the doctor suggested the moment they become aware the thought was negative to visualize a big red stop sign with big, bold, white letters. Focus on the stop sign in your mind until you are able to bring the positive thought to your mind.

I practice the "Stop Sign" exercise regularly. I usually don't have to visualize it for long, for I have a very full "Positive Thought File Cabinet" filled with positive thoughts to take its place. Perhaps you could think of one or two positive thoughts to use as you practice changing your thoughts from negative to positive. Practice these thoughts often so that when you need them they are readily available for you. The more you practice, the easier it becomes. After some time, you could add more positive thoughts to focus on and add to your personal collection of positive thoughts to store in your *own* "Positive Thought File Cabinet".

When I began on my own personal journey, simply being aware of my thoughts was amazing to me. I would notice how often they would go through my mind, and I would say to myself, "Everything you think about is negative." In the beginning, I wouldn't try to change the thoughts. I would just simply make a practice of being aware of them. Upon being aware, I would not "beat myself up" or have a "guilt trip" because of the negativity that was having a party in my mind. No, I would be gentle with myself by knowing those thoughts were all part of my conditioning. This is how I was conditioned from early childhood up until it was permitted that I was allowed to think for myself. Those conditioned thoughts created my life. Those conditioned thoughts were my life up until this particular time where I was now aware of them.

This awareness is exciting! When you are at the awareness moment, you realize these thoughts were NOT your fault and you can learn to manage your thoughts! When you manage your thoughts, your perspectives will change, your choices about so many things will change—and your life will change! Don't you think this is exciting?! Upon learning this, I cannot recall another time I had felt so relieved, free from guilt and with more excitement in all my life. I realized there was some work to be done—yet I was so ready to do the work. The theory is simple yet so understandable! I was beginning to understand myself. I was also beginning to understand more about others and their behaviors and choices. And without sounding too presumptuous, I was beginning to understand a little about human development for the first time in my life.

You see, when you were a baby you were perfect. You didn't have to say anything or do anything to be perfect, you just were. You freely expressed yourself, even when you were angry. When you were upset, everybody knew about it. You were also happy. And when you were happy, everyone seemed to be happy. When you laughed, everyone laughed. Did you know that babies have a high risk of dying if they don't receive enough love? Now you know the reason hospitals often ask for volunteers to come and rock the babies in the neonatal centers.

Once you started to grow, you were taught to live without love, but babies would not put up with living without love. When you were a baby, you loved every part of yourself, your toes, your tummy, everything! Can you believe it!? Yes, at one time you loved every single part of your own body. Then, you started to listen to adults around you who were fearful. And you became fearful and denied all that was amazing about you. And as you continued to grow, your thoughts had a foundation of fear, and these thoughts you heard over and over again throughout your life.

Perhaps you think everyone else has life figured out and you don't.

What happens when these negative thoughts continue? First and foremost, you feel as if you are living life in a prison, or perhaps you think everyone else has life figured out and you don't. In today's world, they might also be shown through obesity, heart disease, chronic fatigue, addictions, etc. Don't you think it is essential to do whatever you can to help yourself learn to change your thoughts to not only live a beautiful life, but to have a healthy physical life as well? I talk to so many people who struggle with being overweight. They spend so much time trying to correct the problem that is not even the real problem. A new diet, a new pill, reading books and magazines on what to eat and how much and what exercises to do to lose the weight. Yet, years later, they are still overweight. The physical weight is only the effect of a more in depth inner problem.

I realized I subconsciously weighed almost a hundred pounds more than what was healthy for me. Consciously I was starting a new diet every time Monday rolled around. The only way I was able to lose weight was when I started working on my negative thoughts. I used to think I couldn't love myself because I was so fat—later I learned I was so fat because I didn't love myself. Why didn't I feel "worthy" enough to love myself? Because of my conditioning. Do I blame those people in my past who were a large part of my development? Well, let me tell you, for years I blamed every single one of them. I was arrogant and "snappy" with my replies. When I was around them, I had an attitude so sharp I could have cut a brick with it! Yet once I learned about blame, I worked very hard to change my attitude.

When I was blaming those people from my past, I had no power.

I learned if I wanted to stay in the problem, I could continue to blame others. When I was blaming those people from my past, I had no power. It was so enlightening to me to learn that my parents were doing the best they could with the awareness, understanding, experience and the knowledge they had. Your parents were doing the best that they could too. We are not taking responsibility for ourselves when we blame others. Those others who did awful things to you were just as scared as you are. They felt helplessness just like you do. The only things any of them could ever possibly teach you is what they had been taught themselves.

When I was asked how much I knew about my parent's childhood, I didn't know much. So I began asking about their lives and was full of compassion when I learned of some of their challenges, their hurts and their fears. I needed the knowledge of their childhoods for my own freedom. What kind of childhood did your parents have? Can you imagine what they must have lived through to become the kind of parent who raised you? You need to know about your parent's childhoods to be able to free them, and in turn, free yourself. Then, and only then when you are able to forgive them, you will be able to forgive yourself. If you say your parents have to be perfect, then you will expect yourself to be perfect too, and you will live a life of misery.

This also goes for others in your past. Perhaps a brother or a sister, an elementary school teacher, a coach or babysitter did or said something that deeply wounded you. This is what they were taught. This is what knowledge, experience, awareness and understanding they had when they did what they did to you. When you become aware and forgive, you will be set free. I am not suggesting you forgive the actions or words spoken of the person; you will most likely always remember the painful action and words. Yet work diligently on forgiving the person.

Most likely you will find "forgiveness" in whatever philosophy or spirituality you personally follow. The reason for this is because it has such a major impact on your life and the lives of others. Many times it is the person you think you would never be able to forgive in this lifetime that is the person you need to forgive the most. If you don't forgive that particular person, that person will not be affected in the least, yet your life will continue to be miserable. They have no pain regarding the issue, only you do.

Many times it is the person you think you would never be able to forgive in this lifetime that is the person you need to forgive the most.

I thank God every day that I found the awareness and strength to forgive those people in my past. The adults who did not nurture me, protect me or teach me, the men who emotionally, physically and sexually abused me since childhood, the teachers who did not choose to see the warning signs of my behavior and just let me pass to the next level, the relationships that manipulated me and used my weaknesses for their own personal gain. But most of all, I am thankful I was able to forgive myself.

I've researched and studied forgiveness for many years. Since I knew it was imperative to my healing, yet I simply couldn't see how I could possibly forgive the people who had wounded me so strongly. I felt I needed to learn as much as I possibly could in the hopes of being able to find the strength to do what must be done. I learned I am incredibly capable. I also learned to accept every part of myself and all of my experiences. I learned it is very healthy for me to understand and be aware that those past painful experiences were in actuality opportunities to learn and to grow. You see, if I hadn't endured such a painful past, I wouldn't be writing a book to assist others with their healing and journey for a beautiful life. Every tear I cried, every hurt I felt, every betrayal I experienced was not in vain. It was through these experiences that I found my truth, my soul. That morning in front of the fireplace was where I found my myself, my purpose.

Reflections
FOR CHAPTER 8

Forgiveness is not only about forgiving those who've wronged you, or who you think have wronged you; it is also about forgiving yourself. What do I mean by that? Sit back for a moment and reflect on any incident when someone hurt you and you thought, *"I can never forgive him/her for what he/she did."* How long did you carry that hurt within you? Somewhere along the way the hurt would have faded. And yet what most of us do in such a situation is simply cling to the I-will-not-forgive feeling, resorting to anger.

Whenever someone wants to mask guilt, resorting to anger is the simplest thing to do. Now, where did guilt come from? Guilt stems from the feeling that you let the person hurt you, that you let the hurt affect you and spent so much of your time agonizing over it. But, by switching to anger, you continue wasting your time over something that you should have left behind a long time ago.

This guilt stops weighing on you only when you let the hurt go, when you forget and forgive. How can you help yourself forgive another? How can you absolve yourself of the guilt and get on with your life? Reflect upon the pointers that come up next; they may give you an answer:

1. Stop thinking of yourself as the sufferer, the martyr, the victim... whatever self-pitying phrase you use for yourself. Get over it! You are what you want to be. You are responsible for what you are and where you go. That person may have hurt you once, but you continue to do so the thousand times you repeat the incident and then sit and wallow in pity.

2. Sometimes, it all boils down to the fact that people are scared of change. You are afraid of forgiving the person because you are afraid of the change your judgment will bring. Change is good, let go…forgiving him/her will set you free.

3. Think of what forgiveness can give you. Only a guiltless heart can truly forgive. Only a brave heart can move on and get over the hurt. You can choose to forgive, just as you can choose not to forgive. Yes, that's what it is all about…the choices you make. There's nothing stopping you from forgiving others and yourself other than you. You can let yourself stay bound to the trauma, hurt and abuse of your past, or forget about it and accept what the future has to bring with a clear mind and a clear heart without experiences of the past to mar your decisions.

Many things in life are about choices, forgiveness being one of them. Choose wisely.

Notes

Notes

Notes

Notes

" Some of the biggest challenges in relationships come from the fact that most people enter a relationship in order to get something: they're trying to find someone who's going to make them feel good. In reality, the only way a relationship will last is if you see your relationship as a place that you go to give, and not a place that you go to take. "

~ANTHONY ROBBINS

Chapter 9

RELATIONSHIPS: THE MAGNIFIER OF JOY

Everything is a relationship. Everything. You have a relationship with the people in your life. You have a relationship with objects, food, nature and all things. All of these relationships mirror the relationship you have with yourself, and the relationship you have with yourself is a result of the relationships you had as a child with the adults who were in your life. How the adults reacted to you when you were a child is most likely the way you act towards yourself now.

How do you scold yourself? Most likely it is the same way your parents scolded you. When they would praise you, what would they say? I bet they are the same words you say to yourself.

What if you were the child who no adult praised? You wouldn't know how to praise yourself, would you? Or perhaps you do not believe there is anything about yourself worth praising. Are you getting a better understanding of the how's and why's of your behavior now? When I learned things such as how I would scold or praise myself and where it derived from, it was a sigh of relief to me. In most cases, every relationship we have is a mirror of the relationship we have had with either our mother or our father. I knew I had to heal those relationships before I would ever be able to create what I wanted in relationships.

In most cases - every relationship we have is a mirror of the relationship we have had with our mother or our father.

I have learned that all the relationships I have obtained in my life were a mirror of myself. What I attracted always mirrored what I knew about relationships. I made many unhealthy choices when it came to the relationships I attracted throughout my life up until that moment in front of the fireplace. Yet, this is what I knew. I am not blaming my parents. Remember, we are all victims of victims. Everyone is doing the best they can with what they know.

All of us attract relationships that mirror us. Our friends, our lovers, our spouse, our boss, our employees are people we attract. If there are things you don't like about the people you attract, that is because their conditioning is the same as your conditioning in some area of their person. The part you don't love.

Let's take for example a friend who is not someone you could trust and disappoints you. Now close your eyes, look deep inside of you and ask yourself "Am I someone I can trust?" Answer honestly. Then ask yourself "Am I willing to remove this part of myself?" When you make a commitment to remove these beliefs from your thoughts, the other person will change or move on from your life.

If you have a lover who is manipulative and cold, look inside yourself and see if one of your parents was manipulative and cold. Perhaps you have a child who has a behavior towards certain things that gets under your skin. I am most certain they are your behaviors. The only way your child can learn is by imitating those adults they are around.

Reprogram your thoughts and remove it from within you, and you will find your child will remove it automatically.

I learned the only way to change others was to change myself. When I changed myself, I changed my life.

A portion of the proceeds of this book goes to the Children's Advocacy Center

Reflections
FOR CHAPTER 9

Remember: *All of us attract relationships that mirror us.* We get along well with people who represent things, values and qualities we hold dear. Here's a small exercise that validates these statements:

Take a sheet of paper and write down the name of a person within your close group of friends. List down things you like about him/her. Now, think of one person you completely dislike. Write down things you don't like about him/her. Also, try and think of one quality you like in that person. You might find it difficult, but no one is 100% bad. Once that's done, turn the sheet over and write your own good and bad qualities on that side.

Now compare your positives with that of your friends. How similar are they? Next, compare your positives with the negatives of the person you dislike; they'll most probably be the opposite of what you hold dear. The one positive that you like in that person will probably figure somewhere in your list of good qualities too.

What did this exercise tell you? You attract people who have similar qualities and values as you. The person you dislike might have friends who like him for what he is, because his qualities and values overlap with theirs.

So, here are the tricks to attracting good relationships:

1. Good grooming and appearance are key to initiating that first contact, but they are not much help beyond that. The best looking people can be the loneliest. How you behave after you've been given that opportunity to forge a relationship is what matters.

2. Treat them as you want to be treated. You can't blow from hot one minute to cold the next. You can't be bubbling and friendly today and dismissive the next. How would you feel if someone were to behave that way to you? Behavior of this sort will only create a sense of mistrust and drive people away.

3. You might want the people you get into relationships with to be perfect. But what about you? What about the flaws you have? Think of what you have to offer to any relationship and work on improving your flaws. Give the best of yourself to others and the best will come to you.

4. Last, and most importantly, be the kind of person you want your friends or those in any sort of relationship with you to be. The vibes you send out will attract the sort of people who complement those vibes.

Getting into relationships is one thing; staying in them is quite another. Are you up for it?

Notes

Notes

Notes

Notes

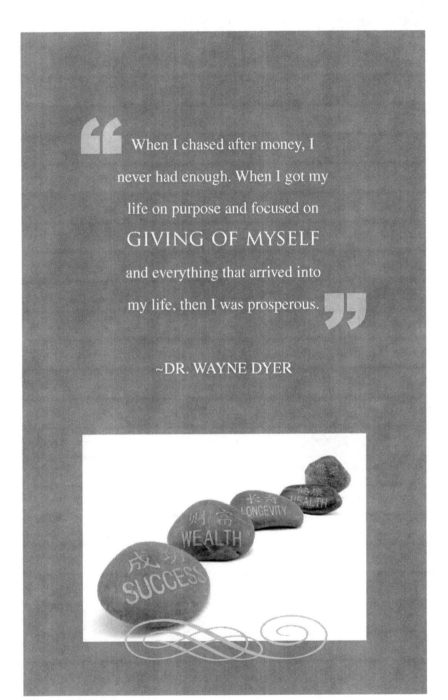

When I chased after money, I
never had enough. When I got my
life on purpose and focused on

GIVING OF MYSELF

and everything that arrived into
my life, then I was prosperous.

~DR. WAYNE DYER

Chapter 10

Removing Your Mental Barriers to Abundance

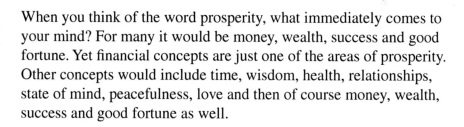

When you think of the word prosperity, what immediately comes to your mind? For many it would be money, wealth, success and good fortune. Yet financial concepts are just one of the areas of prosperity. Other concepts would include time, wisdom, health, relationships, state of mind, peacefulness, love and then of course money, wealth, success and good fortune as well.

Have you ever heard someone say, "There just aren't enough hours in the day." We all have the same amount of hours in our day. No one has more than someone else. Yet, some are more prosperous with their time. Why do you think that is? First of all, if we go around saying things like "I will never have enough time to get everything finished", then guess what? We will be correct.

What about your relationships? Do you feel they aren't full of love, or do you feel they are lacking in many areas? If you are in relationships that are unfulfilling or emotionally unhealthy, it will be difficult for you to attract new relationships that are fulfilling and emotionally healthy. I recall a time in my life when I was in a relationship with a lover that was very unhealthy, and all my relationships with others in my life during this time were very unhealthy as well. Isn't that interesting? This new lover came into my life and he was jealous, manipulative and emotionally draining, and during this time I was attracting friends in other areas of my life who were compulsive liars, conceited and emotionally unstable.

Are you healthy, or are you ill much of the time? Do you have colds and the flu often? Do you have aches and pains? Years ago I was sick all the time. Every winter I would catch a cold and the flu, and on a couple of occasions I was hospitalized for pneumonia. My body ached all the time. I was in physical pain most of my life.

And then of course there is money. Many people say they never have enough money. Do you recall hearing yourself ever say this? What limits have you put on yourself to receive money? Do you believe you are only worth a certain amount? Are you on a fixed income? Who fixed it?

What are your beliefs about money, financial wealth and good fortune? When it comes to money, do you resent others who have more than yourself? Do you believe money only comes from working very hard and for long hours? Do you believe you only deserve to make a certain amount? Do you feel you should only charge a minimal amount for your services? Do you often focus on your debt? Are you afraid you will go broke? Do any of these beliefs hit home with you? Do you think prosperity will come to you with this limited thinking pattern? Where did your beliefs about money come from?

It is imperative to consciously remove your old beliefs before you will be able to live a life of prosperity.

Perhaps you are being offered prosperity and you aren't even noticing it. When someone tried to help me in my past, I would thank them but tell them I could do it myself. Then, in the middle of doing whatever it was, I would think, "Why didn't I graciously accept their offer?" This friend was offering me time prosperity and relationship prosperity, yet during this time in my life I did not feel I deserved it. I would refuse it. Today, I am very aware of the gifts of prosperity presented to me. And I now accept them graciously. I love the old saying, "What comes around, goes around," and today I am enjoying and accepting when it comes around to me. I now realize I deserve good things. Before I realized this I would always have money problems and time management issues—then you know what I would do? I would attract people with the same problems, and we would sit around and complain about it together. The negative vibrations from one area of my life would flow to another area of my life and come around full circle. In the past, my life was filled with so many negative vibrations that it was detrimental for my well being, and I had to consciously make some much needed changes. I needed to clear out the old negative, limiting patterns to make room for the wonderful gifts of prosperity in all areas of my life.

Clear out the old negative, limiting patterns to make room for the wonderful gifts of prosperity

We need to make room in our lives so that when the gifts of prosperity are presented to us, we will have cleared out a space for them. This reminds me of a Saturday morning not so long ago. A friend and I had planned to take a trip to a nearby city to shop and have a leisurely lunch. Upon awakening that morning, I noticed I had a few hours before the time we had planned to depart, so I took my time and enjoyed a long hot bath, styled my hair, took extra time with my makeup, listened to some inspiring music, wrote in my journal, picked out my clothes and then went to my jewelry drawer to choose some fun things to wear. I have a drawer in the top of my dresser that I use just for fun jewelry. There is never anything in there that is really expensive, just colorful and whimsical. I keep it very organized with like colors and combinations of patterns together. As I looked at the jewelry, I noticed many of the pieces were beginning to look worn out. They had come to the end of their fun little lives. So, I found a plastic bag and started to fill it with a lot of the pieces of inexpensive art. I figured I could offer them to an artist friend of mine who would most likely take them apart and use them in some fashion for her art creations. Before I would actually put the worn pieces in the bag, I would really look at them and try to think of the last time I wore them and where. Who was I with? What did we do? What kind of energy was present? Some of the memories were wonderful, and some of the memories were before I had made a shift in my consciousness and were painful. As I would put each piece gently down into the bag, I would kiss the piece and send it away with love. This went on for quite a while. It was quite cleansing. As the drawer became less cluttered, my mind was becoming less cluttered.

Every area of my home is organized and does not have any clutter. If I haven't used an item within six months to a year, it is given away or thrown away. I've had many people say, "You are so lucky! I would love to have a home like yours!" One of the main differences about my house and those who would like to have one like it is my commitment to keep the positive energy flowing throughout every area of my home. I could give you a box of trash bags and tell you to fill them up with "things" you haven't used in the past year from your home and bring them to me, and you would be close to having a home similar to mine. Many people hoard things as if there is not going to be enough and they need to keep all that they can. What a miserable way to live. They keep all their junk and they wonder why new and exciting things are not presented to them. It's because there is no room! Also, they have to maintain all their junk. That would be so very exhausting! Get rid of it! It's only stuff, and it's most likely not worth any monetary value anyway, and if it is, sell it! Make room for new!

My friend arrived at my home that day, and we took off for our Saturday adventure. We decided to visit one store before we went to enjoy our lunch. We walked in, and right in front of me was an abundance of displays featuring bright, shiny, new, colorful and whimsical jewelry. And above each display, a bright red sign read, "Saturday Jewelry Sale—75% Off"! I made room for the new, and it was presented to me within hours. And to think we hadn't even planned to go into that particular store that day. Traffic had been very good that morning, so we arrived earlier than planned, and it wasn't quite time to eat lunch, so we just happened upon the store and decided to go take a look. This type of positive energy comes to me daily. When I need something, it's there. When I think about something I want, it is presented to me in one way or another. When I am lonely, the perfect friend shows up. Upon changing my conscious belief patterns, this is the way of my world.

It was difficult for me to accept that I was the only person responsible for my lack of prosperity. I didn't think I deserved it. I didn't think I was good enough to receive it. I thought that my life was mapped out and this was just how it was suppose to be. I wasn't one of the lucky ones. I wasn't one of the talented and beautiful people. As long as I kept these thoughts in my mental being, I lacked prosperity.

Our exterior reality is a reflection of our inner beliefs.

Remember, our exterior reality is a reflection of our inner beliefs. Whatever we think our world is supposed to be for us becomes our reality. When we change our inner thinking patterns, we can change our external reality. It's very simple.

What is important to you? Really think about this. Perhaps what is important for you may not be necessarily important for someone else. What are the things you want and the ability to enjoy them? Do you want an abundant supply of money? Really think about this before you answer. Do you think money is going to fulfill you in every way? Money gives us the power to have material things and to do physical activities, but if some of your most authentic desires are things money can't buy, then no amount of money is going to bring you prosperity. Perhaps you are thinking of money so you can buy other people lots of wonderful things and opportunities. Is that the only reason? What about things for yourself? Do you realize you deserve things too? Do you realize you may even deserve them first? Simply determining what is important for you to obtain your personal level of prosperity is halfway towards obtaining it. You must know what you want before you are able to attract it. If you don't know, how would you recognize it when it shows up?

Once you determine what is important to you, then it is time to determine what your limiting beliefs are about this area. If it is indeed money, think of the patterns you were taught about money. Let the thoughts come into your mind, acknowledge them, then let them go and replace them with new, positive, healthy thoughts. Perhaps thoughts such as, *"Money comes to me in miraculous ways and I am so grateful for all that I have."* Everything you say and think is an affirmation and will create your life. Be very aware of your thoughts and your words and keep them positive. When negative thoughts come up, just simply be aware they are there and release them.

Always be honest. When you are not honest with yourself, it means you do not believe you deserve good things. For example, if you steal pens or stamps from your place of employment, it is as if you are saying, "I don't believe I am good enough to obtain these on my own." If you think you are going to get ahead by not being honest, you will live an unfulfilling life of misery.

Another important channel to prosperity is your gratitude. Look around you and think of the things you are grateful for. As you go throughout your day, be aware of all the wonderful people, things and opportunities you are grateful for. We all have so many wonderful things in our life right at this very moment, but all too often we choose to ignore it. You will not attract more to be grateful for if you ignore what you already have.

An exercise I enjoy every day is sitting with my arms open wide and saying, "I am open to receiving all that is good from God." Try it! You may feel somewhat silly at first, yet continue this exercise and notice how wonderful it feels. I wouldn't miss a day without opening myself up to all the wonderful gifts of prosperity that are presented to me daily.

Reflections FOR CHAPTER 10

In order to achieve prosperity, you first need to get rid of your negative affirmations about prosperity and more specifically money. If you go around thinking that wanting more money than what you have is bad, evil or unspiritual, you'll never end up attracting money. Think of it as a form of energy. If energy can flow to you, why not money?

I've mentioned some of the ways you can attract prosperity into your life. Here are some more:

1. *Imagine*: Imagination is a very strong and vital force. Imagine what you'd do if you had the prosperity you crave. Make images in your mind. Your subconscious catches on to those images and helps you work towards them.

2. *Stay clear of debts*: Debts and the worries they bring with them can give your subconscious negative ideas about money. Try and stay away from incurring debts. The less your debts, the less stressed you will be and the more money you will attract.

3. *Make a list of things you are grateful for*: This helps you know that you have so much to be thankful for. Writing channels and focuses your energy. Know what prosperity you enjoy and thank the universe or God, whichever one you believe in for giving it to you. Then add things that you'd like to receive and be grateful for.

4. *Why do you want prosperity?* Do some thinking about why you want the prosperity you want. As I've said before, simply wishing for things is not going to help. Asking relevant questions and chalking out a plan to answer them tunes in your subconscious.

5. *Meditate*: Fix a time either early in the morning or when you go to bed, to spend a few minutes meditating over what you have and what you want in the minutest detail. See yourself in the life you want. See yourself enjoying that life. It might not be easy initially. Calm your mind's jabber by taking in a few deep breaths. *Believe you've got the prosperity you want even before you receive it.*

6. *Work towards it*: All this visualization, meditation and imagination may come to naught unless you work towards achieving the prosperity you want. Nothing appears out of thin air. You'll need to put in effort to get the requisite results.

You hold the key to your prosperity. Prosperity awaits you...you only need to look for it. Do not limit yourself; ask for it and let it come.

Notes

Notes

Notes

Notes

> Those who haven't seen me in years often say 'Oh my goodness, you don't look like the same person!' I usually give them a hug and pat their back as I lightly whisper in their ear, 'I'm not.'

~LISA HARDWICK

Broken
Diagnosed with severe clinical depression, post traumatic stress syndrome and morbid obesity.

Beautiful
Living an authentic beautiful life.

Chapter 11

MY STORY: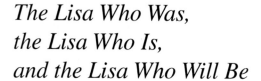
The Lisa Who Was,
the Lisa Who Is,
and the Lisa Who Will Be

I surprise my mom when I bring up things about my childhood and they are memories from when I was under two years of age. I really have the ability to remember things very clearly. Like exactly the layout of the house, the people that would come and visit, the color of the drapes, where we kept the Christmas ornaments. Many people would think I was fortunate to be able to remember so far back and in detail, like it was a gift. Yet all my life, it was very painful to remember. I carried grief and shame in my heart from my earliest memories.

My mother gave birth to me when she was sixteen years old. My father was sixteen as well. They had married in my grandparent's living room when my mother was pregnant. Any little girl brought into this world under those conditions most likely would feel she was a mistake. It is well known when my father first saw me he cried out, "Oh God, she's so ugly!" This was brought up often at family get-togethers. My father also said my mother became pregnant on purpose to trap him into marrying her yet the fact is he forced her to have sex with him and she became pregnant. Babies can sense if they are wanted or not. I was a mistake.

Six months before I was born, my uncle was born to my paternal grandmother. He was the focus for any child attention. I received what was left over. I think my grandmother resented me for being a girl because she had wanted one so bad. Not that this was indeed the case, yet this is how I *perceived* it to be. My uncle and I spent most of our toddler lives together. I adored him, yet he never wanted much to do with me. He was just imitating what he was shown. He probably doesn't even realize it to this day how much I thought of him. He was an awesome little kid, yet he just didn't like me. There is an old family movie of him and me walking down the street. I am trying to hold his hand, and he is smacking my hand away. Years later when we gather to watch the old movies and that clip is shown, everybody laughs, yet my heart still breaks. If I was an adult who had the proper care and nurturing, that movie would have been funny. I needed someone to love me. I wanted him to love me. I needed to feel loved.

When I was three, my brother was born. I loved him. I remember just wanting to take care of him and play with him. Not long after he was born, we moved to a big farmhouse in the country. My father was cash renting a farm where he raised corn and beans and we had farm animals. My job was to gather the eggs and help my mother in the house. My parents' marriage was not a healthy relationship. It was filled with emotional and physical abuse, which my brother and I witnessed on a regular basis. My father drank, committed adultery with my mother's best friend, hit her, yelled, screamed, threw things, you name it, we saw it. My mother put up with it, because she loved him. My brother and I had no idea this behavior wasn't *normal*.

At the age of four was the beginning of my first sexual abuse encounter. I hadn't even started kindergarten yet, and I was being molested by a person my family trusted. I would encounter this person a couple of times per week, and each and every time, the manipulative games resulted in sexual hell. This person knew exactly what he was doing. These people prey on little girls who have not been nurtured and are lonely. He was very good at playing his game. He always won.

I went to school at a small country school. I could read before I went to kindergarten. I was doing algebra for show and tell in second grade. I was a bright child. In the middle of my second grade year, a meeting was set up at my home where two gentlemen came to speak to my parents about sending me to a gifted school in Chicago. My dad decided not to let me go.

The summer right before my third grade year, the sexual abuse became advanced. When I look back at that eight year old girl, I can't help but weep for her. She had no choice but to continue this game of hell. She was told things would happen to her and her family if "our secret" ever got out. I walked into my third grade class now as an obese child. I recall the first week we were measured and weighed. The teacher read the weight of each student out loud. I remember when she read my name she said, "Lisa, you weigh 96 pounds. You weigh almost 20 pounds more than everyone else. You need to lose some weight!" I didn't even realize I was obese. I didn't "feel" anything. I look back at pictures of myself around this time and I was so swollen. My little body was swollen, my face was swollen. I was stuffing feelings with food. I had no other way to cope. I had no outlet. I just didn't want to feel anything, ever. I had to do whatever I could to not feel anything. My drug of choice at that very young age was obviously food.

During these early school years, when I did have the opportunity to play with other children one on one, I remember always being willing to play "doctor" or something where we would get undressed. Children are interested and want to explore—yet I would always be the one to suggest going beyond the innocent child's play. This was what I knew. This was how I was conditioned.

In the large country home we lived in, I spent much of my time upstairs away from everyone, in my bedroom closet surrounded by my dolls, stuffed animals and books. A pull chain to a light bulb was my secondary energy. I realize now the time spent in this little space was the way I protected myself. I would spend hours in this little closet reading, setting up everything just so, sneaking food and talking with "my friends".

I recall how sensitive I was to matters. Just everyday conversations with others seemed to lodge tears in my throat. I realize now how deep my negative subliminal programming must have been developing at this very young age. While struggling through these early childhood years, I would be devastated because very often I would return from school where I wet my pants. I would be in so much trouble from my mom and dad. My father would sometimes spank me with a yard stick. I had no control over this problem. Later, my parents decided to take me to a doctor where it was revealed I had some urinary bladder problems and had to be hospitalized a few times to correct the matter. With all of the obvious symptoms of depression, weight gain and infection, it is unfortunate that no one was able to determine the underlying cause of these ailments.

What other child experienced a life such as mine? My research revealed that many lived a very similar life. More than you could ever imagine. I wonder what life they are living now. I am making it my life's mission to educate parents, teachers and doctors on the signs to look for so no other child will have to further endure this personal hell. Did you know today's research says 1 in 4 girls will be sexually abused before they reach the age of 18? People need to be aware! Laws need to be more strict. In my opinion, if a person sexually abuses or abuses a child in any way, they should receive a life penalty the same as if they were a murderer, because in my opinion they did take a precious life.

The summer before fourth grade, my young world fell apart again. I was sexually abused again by another trusting adult while spending the night away from home . I can still recall the scents of alcohol and Old Spice. To this day I cannot fathom the smell of that putrid scent of that disgusting cologne (amazing how our senses bring back fond and painful memories). My mother left my father when she was 25 and we moved to a 2 bedroom bungalow where she slept on the couch so we could have our own bedrooms, and I was told by my paternal grandmother that my brother and I were no longer accepted by my paternal family because of what "my mother had done"—all those grandparents, aunts and uncles and cousins I believed were no longer going to be a part of my brother's and my life. My maternal grandmother, who I loved with all my heart, passed away suddenly while napping on her couch. We lost her at a very young age. I started a new school, and at the age of 10 years old, started my period. I had a different life, different surroundings and was carrying around an enormous amount of guilt, shame, resentment and despair.

My father would promise to pick us up for visits, yet most of the time when he was expected to arrive for our weekend visit, he would conveniently forget. I still recall my little brother sitting on the porch wearing his little baseball hat and resting his BB gun on his lap, stretching his little neck hoping to catch a view of my father's truck coming to take him "home" for the weekend. On the rare occasion he would show, most of the time he would just take my brother. On the more rare occasion he would actually allow me to visit him, it was to clean his bachelor pad, wash all his dishes, vacuum his house and empty his ashtrays. The moment his home was back in order, he returned me to town to my mother.

I no longer blame my father. He was doing what he knew. His childhood was a series of his father not coming home on a regular basis also. My father was doing the best he could with how he had been taught. Knowing that we were all doing the best we could with what we knew certainly helped my healing. Our father was going through his own pain. Perhaps it was painful to see us. Perhaps he was doing his best to cope by running around in his Corvette, dating lots of women and frequenting the local taverns trying to numb his own pain. I'm certain that is why he couldn't love us the way we needed to be loved. My future self attempted these very same methods of numbing pain as well.

During this stressful period in my life, I was responsible for much of the care of my younger brother. Sometimes we were left alone . The home my mother had rented was in the college student district, so there were always parties and such going on in the neighborhood in the evenings. I recall sleeping upright against the front door with a kitchen knife, scared to death someone was going to try to break in and hurt my brother and me. Some nights I didn't sleep at all . Now I look back and realize it was simply very strong anxiety.

In the fourth grade at my new elementary school, my teacher approached me one afternoon after she found a note I had written to a boy. "Lisa, you are boy crazy and it is not appropriate at this age." I will remember that embarrassing conversation forever. I was simply looking for what I knew—a male to give me attention and perhaps hurt me—for this is what I was taught as "love" from a male.

The first time I realized I was different from my peers was during the first week of junior high school. I must have been around twelve or thirteen years old. The kids were coming to school with certain styles of clothes, particular brands and hairstyles. I wore the same pants every day. I was so overweight it was difficult to find clothes to fit me, and money was scarce for such things as proper school attire. My mother actually qualified for food stamps but was too proud to accept them . I was starting to be made fun of a lot in school. "Fat pig", "Fat ass", "You stink." I heard them all. I most likely wasn't using the best of hygiene back then. No one had ever taught me. I remember during one of the visits to my dad's house he looked right at me and said, "You stink! Go take a bath!" I am sure I did stink. I can imagine the negative self-talk I experienced during that bath. I was embarrassed and ashamed. I would always think, "What is wrong with me!? Why can't I just get it right? I don't think I will ever be able to make my mom or dad happy, they will never love me." During that period in junior high school, I would fantasize about dying. What child does this? Perhaps a child who has been sexually abused, lost their favorite grandmother, her parents just divorced, she is addicted to food and is clinically obese, she is scared and she feels unloved. Yeah, I can understand what kind of child would fantasize about dying.

I portrayed a "fantasy family life" to my classmates. I spent years with them, and I kept my secrets concealed. I already didn't fit in, so if they were to find out about my "real" life, I was certain I would endure more ridicule and teasing at school. I hated it when I would enter the school cafeteria and the boy's table would make "mooing" sounds to show me they thought I was like a cow. My classmates most likely knew my parents were divorced, yet I would never let them know that many times we were worried about paying the light bill, I hadn't slept the night before, I had an adult that I was helping live out his sexual fantasies, and I was terrified and lonely. It was a full time job wearing that heavy mask all those years since elementary school. I came up with the most amazing, outlandish stories about family vacations, people my parents "knew", what we had and what our plans were. All to fit in. All to belong. All to bring some kind of comfort from being so terrified someone would find out the real story.

I was promiscuous through childhood and more so in high school. At the age of thirteen, I fell in love with a twenty-one-year-old man. He was my world. He was handsome, had bright blue eyes, a Leif Garrett hairstyle and an amazing personality. I would do anything to be able to see him. I told my mother more lies than I can count to be able to be with him. I would spend the night with a girlfriend, and then leave their home in the middle of the night just to spend the night with him.

I would never tell my girlfriends that I was doing more than kissing him. I experienced firsthand how we young girls handled such news. It would have been all over town by the next day. And my fear was that my parents would find out and I would never see him again. Needless to say, we all know why a twenty-one-year-old man was interested in a thirteen-year-old young girl with low self-esteem. He ended up moving away, and I didn't think my heart would ever mend. This guy played an emotional and manipulative game with me to get what he wanted, but I didn't care because "this game" felt wonderful. I was now addicted to the feeling of this "high" of "being in love".

By the time I started high school, my mother had remarried. My stepfather was a man who had been in my life since I was about eight years old. He had never had children, and now he was an instant father to two children, one being more "broken" than he could ever know. Boy, did I put this man through hell. He allowed me to have a birthday party when I was thirteen years old in his nice home, in a nice neighborhood as long as it was in the GARAGE. No kids were to be in the house, and it was to be limited to twenty people only. Believe me when I say my stepfather will never forget that party. He still brings it up even though we do chuckle about it today. The party ended up with about fifty kids, as well as my stepfather and mother busy answering the front door most of that evening, letting the Harley riders that came to join in the fun know there was no "adult" party here. Yeah, I was quite a handful to my stepfather. During these first years in high school, my mother and I did not get along at all. I remember coming home from school and sleeping. I slept a lot. Looking back, it was most certainly signs of depression. I couldn't concentrate in school, I couldn't concentrate at home. I would numb myself with food, alcohol, cigarettes and relationships.

By the end of my sophomore year, my father had also remarried. His wife was a very caring person, and she had a daughter, Heather Miller, who was about four years old. Heather was an adorable little girl with very light blonde hair who followed me around and made me feel adored. My father said he wanted his family back together, so my brother moved in with him and later I did as well. But the Brady Bunch façade didn't last long. He was very strict and was emotionally abusive to all of us. He was raising his family the way he was conditioned. He never gave me any positive reinforcement or attention like he had implied he would when I agreed to move in with him and his new family.

One afternoon after I got off the school bus, my dad told me that after dinner that evening, he had a surprise for me. The day had finally come, I thought. I was going to receive something from my dad because he must have figured out I was really special and he got something just for me! I hurried and did my chores...cleaning the pig lots, feeding the chickens, gathering the eggs, helping my stepmother with dinner. I felt as excited as a kid getting ready to go to Disney World!

Finally we all sat down at the table. I always would smirk to myself when I would hear people say, "Dinner time as a family is one of the most important times of a family's day." Really? Our dinner time was always spent together as a family, and it usually ended up with something dramatic happening. You never knew what mood Dad or any of the family members were going to be in during dinner time. I've seen an entire table with all the food, plates, silverware and glasses be flung across the room because the salt and pepper weren't on the table. So I will have to disagree with dinner time being so important for ALL families. But something like this was not going to happen tonight. I was very careful to watch everyone's body language, and when my brother wanted to pick on me, I didn't take the bait. No one was going to ruin this dinner. This was going to be a special night; I was going to make sure of it.

Dinner was winding down, and my stepmother and I started cleaning the table while my brother and stepsister prepared to leave the room. Dad directed all of us to stop doing what we were doing and to come sit back down. He had a surprise for "Sissy". "Sissy" was what he usually called me when he wanted something or when he treated me so badly that after a while I felt his guilt had gotten the best of him. I am certain his father had a pet name for him too when he was a child. We all sat patiently. He cleared an area directly in front of where he was sitting. I remember looking at my stepmother for some kind of hint of what the surprise might be, yet she looked at me with a facial expression that said she really didn't know. My dad told me to walk downstairs to the basement and on the landing there would be a brown bag.

"Don't look in it. Just bring it up and put it here in front of me", he said.

So I did as I was told, and when I got to the bottom of the stairs, I saw the bag and picked it up. "Rural King" was written on the bag. I walk back up the stairs, giggling and rolling my eyes at the same time. Well, at least he tried, I thought.

He motioned for me to set the bag in front of him as he told everyone at the table, "Now, sit still...I want you to see this".

He told me to pull out what was in the bag. I reached in and felt something soft, some kind of clothing. I pulled it out and saw it was a pair of dark blue, draw-stringed sweat pants.

He said, "Hold them up so everyone can see."

You know how huge those draw-stringed sweat pants look? Oh yeah, these looked huge.

"These are for you, Sissy. Now every day after you get off the school bus, you are going to jog your BIG FAT ASS up to the end of the road and back until you lose some of that goddamn weight!" Tears welled up in my eyes. I couldn't believe this was happening to me. I stood there with my mind spinning. I heard sounds in the background…my brother hitting the table with his fist, laughing hysterically, my stepsister sniffling like she was about to cry, my stepmother clearing the table quickly like she was nervous again. This was my life. How in the world was my future self ever expected to be attracted to a man who would be good to me when this was what I was taught "love" was? And if my future partner did treat me well, perhaps I would do things so he wouldn't treat me well so I would be comfortable due to my conditioning. Or maybe, just maybe, the future guy would just pack up and go. Yeah, this is what I was taught to be looking for in the future.

Every day I would try my best to run up to the end of the road and back. I would start walking, then jogging, then walk again, then run. Almost every day I would do this with tears running down my face. Just like the tears that are flowing down my face right at this moment as I write this painful memory. I didn't lose weight; I just ate more to numb the pain. This went on until it was winter and it began snowing and blowing. Then Dad just sort of forgot about it.

The next spring came, and I was hoping he wouldn't remember about the running. I hated it. My legs hurt, there was so much weight pounding down on my joints my knees would ache terribly. I didn't even know how to run, regulate my breathing, etc. My dad and my brother were natural athletes. They knew this stuff. I didn't…and I didn't want to learn. When spring would come, we would always start a huge garden. I hated this too. I was too overweight, too out of shape, and I just wanted to be left alone in my room where it was safe and no one would hurt me with my books, food and the few packs of cigarettes I took out of my dad's nightstand.

There were other painful times as well. The time we went to a county fair in Arthur, Illinois, which was about twenty miles or so from our farm. We went to watch my brother and uncle show livestock. At about 10:00 pm, my dad and I started heading back. We had only been on the road for a short time when Dad turned down this country lane. At the end of this lane was a tavern.

He got out and said, "Sissy, I'm going to have you drive the truck home. Just keep heading southeast. You'll find home."

I didn't even have a driver's license. It was dark and I was scared to death. I made it home. I have no idea how he got home or when, and I didn't care.

Or the time we were working in the garden and I asked Dad if I could go see my mom that weekend. I hadn't seen my mom for some time, and I had talked to her that day on the phone. She asked when I was going to come and visit next.

Dad replied, "No, you're not going to go see that b____!" (or something similarly vulgar to this).

I was enraged and yelled at him for the first time in my life, "Don't EVER talk about my mom like that again!"

Everything was quiet for a moment. I bent down to pick up the potatoes my father had dug up, when all of a sudden I saw something from my peripheral vision, and then I felt a pain like I had never felt before. My father had taken a full swing with the potato fork he was using and had hit me as hard as he could on my upper butt and lower back. My body flew into the air, and I landed on my side. The blow was so powerful I wet my pants without even realizing it. I laid there for a while. I didn't care if he beat me to death. Back then, I wished he would have so I would not have to continue to live in this hell. "Get up and go change your pants" was all he said.

To this day, he says he just hit me on the butt in the garden for mouthing off. That was not how it happened. I will never forget this day for as long as I live. Every time I think about it I well up with tears. Since writing this one paragraph, I've had to leave my computer twice to compose myself. There's nothing like tears to cleanse the soul, right? I will always be on a healing journey, yet each and every day I continue to heal, and it feels so much better than the day before.

Now that I know what I know about past conditioning, I can't help but wonder how many times he was manipulated in his childhood and how many times he was hit. The part of me that has such a caring heart feels very sorry for the young man he once was. The other part of me feels pity for him because he could have had an amazing, young, beautiful, talented daughter, but he didn't know how to love her, nurture her and most importantly—protect her. His daughter was broken. Broken into a million little pieces. It would take a miracle to put this mess back together again. Little did anyone know, I would find that miracle.

A few months later, I ran away from home. My girlfriend helped me get together some of my personal belongings in the middle of a Saturday afternoon. I moved back in with my mom. My poor stepfather—he had no idea what he was getting ready to have to deal with. I wasn't a bad kid, I was a broken kid. It was his house and his rules and I was rebellious. I think I was grounded the majority of the time I lived in his and my mom's home.

After many failed teenage relationships, I started dating around my junior year the guy who would become my husband. He was two years older than myself and was the first guy I felt would be a person who would be a good husband and father to our children. We married two months after I graduated high school. He was a very hard worker. We had our first child within that first year. I had no idea how to take care of a baby, yet I did the best I could with what I knew. My son was amazing, adorable and smart.

Problems started in the marriage. My son and I spent time in the coalition against domestic violence. I believe I was just as much to blame as my husband was. I was full of drama. I was not an easy wife to have, and he was bull headed enough to try to put me in my place. The police department most certainly knew who we were. We went to counseling and tried our best to work things out between us. During this time I became pregnant with twins. They were born 3 months premature. The twins were such fighters. They came home separately a few weeks later, and we were told our smallest twin had cerebral palsy. This was a very difficult time for us. I had three children under the age of 3 ½ and a husband who worked on the road for a living. My days were filled with just me, the children and my self-talk.

I found out later my husband had an affair with my best friend, my maid of honor, the woman who helped me move away from my dad. It all seemed more than I could bear, and I was hospitalized for depression and alcohol abuse.

I met a man in rehab and ended up leaving my husband for him. I had no idea how to be a wife or a mother. I knew there was something wrong with me, yet I just didn't know what to do about it. I ended up divorcing my husband, and he met another woman and married her. She was the caregiver to my children when they were very young, and even though not all parents are perfect, she did a pretty good job stepping up to the plate when my boys' mother was running around trying to find herself. I married the man I met in rehab. He came from an awesome family. His parents still visit my sons at Christmas and send them birthday cards some twenty plus years later. Yet, this marriage didn't last either. Two people right out of rehab with brokenness to boot. I'm surprised it lasted almost three years.

I was in and out of hospitals, treatment centers and still taking more antidepressant and anxiety medications than I could count. I struggled with my weight, ranging anywhere from well over two hundred pounds down to one hundred and twenty then back up again. I had been anorexic, bulimic and a compulsive overeater. I tried to numb myself with food, with control, with alcohol, marijuana and with relationships, lots and lots of relationships. Nothing seemed to bring me happiness; nothing seemed to bring me peace or take away the pain.

I married for the third time when I was twenty-eight years old. I was with this person for over twelve years. We had problems before we even were married, yet we both gave the marriage as much effort as we could in the best ways we knew how to. Later in the marriage we had two of my sons living with me, and my third son came to visit quite often. It was his fourth marriage and my third. We had a blended family and owned a small business together. Many assumed this marriage had no chance, yet we lasted for over twelve years. He struggled with my prescriptions, my depression, and my weight issues, and I struggled with his controlling behavior, his anger and the fact that I did not feel loved. I had married what I was taught love was, and the pain continued.

Toward the end of our marriage, I worked as a builder/developer consultant on a large development out of state. I had earned an excellent reputation for assisting builders, developers and investors with their projects. I decided while I was away that I wanted a divorce; I wasn't happy and I just wanted out. The stress of everything was overwhelming. Worrying about things at home, being responsible for a multi-million dollar project, fighting with him on the phone—I was just ready to hang it up again. We ended up divorcing. He kept the house; I left with some cash and another notch on my belt of another failed marriage.

I had met a gentleman while I was working on the project who was also going to get a divorce. Our friendship blossomed into a deeper love than I had ever experienced. We had so much in common. I was head over heels in love…and lust. I found myself totally addicted to him and to the sex. We experienced things together that would make a prostitute blush. A few months into the relationship, this dream man I had found started showing his true colors. He would become possessive and jealous, asking me where I had been and who I had been with. He questioned my every move. During a dinner with friends one evening at a restaurant during a cold winter storm, I looked up at a window and saw him standing outside watching me. There would be many times I would return to my condo at the development and find that he destroyed it, throwing things everywhere—even the items out of the refrigerator. The condo would be ransacked...because I was late.

One night I came home to my condo and all the lights were off in the home, which was strange; I always kept a light on. As I walked into the kitchen, he was sitting in the corner, in the dark, waiting for me. "Where the f___ have you been!"

Earlier that same night, I had been at an appointment with a builder and his wife that he had set up. On my way home, I knew I was coming home later than I had anticipated. It was raining, there was no cell service in this area with winding roads and drop off cliffs, and it was so dark I could barely see the road. I was hurrying because I didn't want to be late and have him upset. My tires met the gravel on the side of the road, and I almost lost control right next to a cliff.

I slowed down and said to myself, "Lisa, there is a problem when you almost kill yourself because you are afraid of what his behavior will be if you're late". In that moment, my heart was beating so fast. I was just inches from a terrible accident.

When I walked into my dark house later that night, something didn't feel right—and it wasn't.

"Where the f___ have you been?!" was what I heard before I adjusted my eyes enough to see him.

I responded that I had almost killed myself trying to get home in time so he wouldn't be flipping out—and tonight I really didn't want to hear it.

This was the wrong thing to say. He again trashed the house right in front of me, took his fist and punched a hole in the drywall, then picked up an expensive golf club I had given him for Christmas and broke it in half with his bare hands. As I went to him to try to calm him down, he threw me across the room. I was airborne for what felt like forever. I had attracted more drama into my life again. I look back now, and it was if I just seemed to expect it.

This relationship was filled with manipulation, drama and abuse, and I was addicted to all of it. This guy was cocky and arrogant and always had a way of twisting words around to make you feel as bad as he obviously did about himself. I know his childhood was full of disappointments and abuse as well, and the mask he wore in front of all of the other businessmen he worked with was as heavy as the one I wore. When I introduced him to family and friends, they were all very worried about this guy. They sensed something—yet the way I was conditioned, I didn't know how to sense anything. I just figured we would work on our problems and everything would eventually work out. It never did, yet the more he would manipulate and abuse me, the more I seemed to be attached to him. He would leave to go see his daughters about every three weeks, and when he would leave my driveway, I would watch him drive away and think, "This is it, and I'm going to end it. He is crazy." But, after a couple of days, I would be weeping for him. I later learned these are the symptoms of many abused women.

Our biggest arguments came when I would ask him about the status of his divorce. I would ask him if he was really just going to see his daughters or if he was seeing his wife. He would get furious every time I brought this up. He told me he hated his wife, yet he had to get some financial things in order. I was starting to wonder. All the beautiful cards, love letters, dates to my favorite theatres, vacations, jewelry, romantic gifts and dinners were not worth the emptiness I was starting to feel. I wanted out, but I didn't know how. I didn't want the pain of him not being there, yet I didn't want the pain when he was there. Then one evening at 9:48

pm on a Thursday night, my phone rang. I was certain it was him calling because the caller ID displayed the area code he called me from quite often. It wasn't. It was his wife.

"What relationship do you have with him?" she demanded.

I asked her who this was.

"It's his WIFE!" she yelled into the phone.

"You mean soon to be ex-wife," I replied.

"No, not ex-wife, we've never talked about a divorce, yet I just read emails you two have been sending back and forth."

I am thankful I had one of my very best friends spending the evening with me that particular night. Because I literally fell apart. Another manipulative man had used me for his own personal gain. Another abusive man had stripped me of more self-esteem. Another unhealthy person who I had attracted into my life. This was it; I was ready to end my life.

For the next few days I didn't eat, shower or sleep. I hurt for myself. I hurt for his wife. My friend, Barbara Simmons, was an amazing caregiver. I was so confused about life. Was this how it was suppose to be? It seemed since birth bad things happened to me constantly. I was never happy for very long, and I was absolutely never at peace. Even when I was in church, I couldn't find any peace. Why did my life seem so much harder than everyone else's life? Almost every day since I could remember, my nerves were shot because of one thing or another. I wanted to be happy; I wanted everyone in the world to be happy. Life was crap. I hated it. I hated God. I hated myself.

One morning after many days of grieving, I lay in front of my fireplace and, as you read in my introduction, I had an awakening.

A true awakening. A shift in my consciousness—and my life would never be the same again. I did not realize at the time that my final breaking point would be my greatest gift, and a gift to many others who struggle with the affects of childhood sexual abuse or any abuse and neglect and the life many lead thereafter.

One of the first steps I took was to research areas of my life. What I found was astounding. For example, in regards to being born to young teenage parents, I learned Medical Journals for Pediatric and Adolescent Medicine all state something similar: Poverty, inadequate social support, mothers' lack of education, mothers' cognitive immaturity, and greater maternal stress have all been suggested as possible factors contributing to poor social and educational outcomes for the children of teen mothers.

Prevention and Early Intervention Centers throughout the United States have data that suggests this special class of children, when compared to children born to adult mothers, are at greater risk for a variety of developmental problems.

As they grow, these children tend to suffer poorer health, and according to parents' reports, only 38% of children born to the youngest adolescent mothers were rated in "excellent" health. These children are at greater risk of being "indicated cases" of child abuse or neglect. Children born to mothers age 15 and younger are two times more likely to become an indicated case of child abuse/neglect in the first five years of their lives than children born to adult mothers.

The children of adolescent mothers are at higher risk for problems in aggressive behavior. Children of adolescent mothers are more likely to drop out of high school when compared to the children born to adult mothers. Only 77% of children born to adolescent mothers complete high school by early adulthood, compared to 89% of the comparison group.

One researcher looked at the incarceration rates of the sons of young mothers. His findings revealed that 10.3% of those born to mothers age 17 and younger were incarcerated, compared to 3.8% of those sons born to adult mothers. This shows that the sons of adolescent mothers are three times more likely to be incarcerated than those born to adult mothers.

The daughters of adolescent mothers are significantly more likely to give birth themselves before the age of 18. A study conducted of the National Longitudinal Survey of Youth date showed that early childbearing is much more common among the daughters of these young mothers, and these daughters are more susceptible than their mothers to economic dependence and most likely will continue to live in poverty.

Overall, children born to teen mothers often do not have a fair starting field. They are more likely to grow up in poverty and in a single parent home and to experience high risks to both health and potential education achievement.

MY "Ah Ha" Moment: Upon taking personal responsibility to research children of adolescent parents, I started to understand the whys and the hows. These disadvantages were a result of my conditioning. Just knowing that I was up against some really tough odds in my past gave the realization that I am very strong. I was strong enough to still be standing, and I am strong enough to work hard to heal the pain those disadvantages caused.

I then researched further the effects of childhood sexual abuse and learned from the Survivors of Incest Anonymous, Inc. any sexual contact between a child and a trusted individual will result in scarring virtually all facets of the victim's life, since she is left with little or no self-esteem.

At least one out of six boys and one out of four girls will be abused before they turn 18. The child's emotional growth will be stifled at the age of the first attack, and the victim most likely will not recover until adulthood, if in fact they ever do.

Arising from incest are alcoholism, drug addiction, promiscuity and even prostitution. Eating and/or sleeping disorders, migraines, back or stomach pains are just a few of the symptoms victims may suffer from. Food, sex, alcohol and/or drugs help to stuff painful memories of the abuse temporarily. If a victim believes that obesity is unattractive, and if she believes she was abused because she was beautiful, she may subconsciously overeat in a misguided attempt to defend herself from being assaulted again. Anorexia is another form of self-punishment, which eventually leads to self-victimizing oneself and results in suicide.

The emotional problems created from the abuse include the inability to trust, perfectionism, phobias and avoidance of both intimacy and emotional bonding. The victim used a denial system as her survivor method as a child, and now that particular method prevents her from enjoying a free life. She was forced to become an expert in disbelieving her own senses, therefore she doesn't trust her own perceptions. She convinces herself she overreacted, nothing really bad happened or perhaps they were just playing. Her reality is too painful for a child's mind, so she learns to fictionalize. It is painful to give up a fantasy life, since children think of themselves as either a blessing or a disgrace. So, she makes excuses for the abuser such as "he was drunk" or "he had a bad childhood himself". She ends up blaming herself. If she continues to use these ways to cope as she grows into adulthood, she is set up to be in an abusive relationship. In Survivors of Incest Anonymous, she can learn to accept the fact that she was abused rather than loved. She can then learn to seek out only healthy relationships.

The victim may have problems with parenting and always wondering if her decisions are right. Victims may at times avoid parenting all together, or try to be the perfect parent. The worst possible consequence is when a victim abuses the next generation.

An experiment was conducted in which dogs were forced to experience hurtful electrical shocks without any means of escape. A second group of dogs were given shocks and when possible quickly escaped. When the first group was shocked again and escape was possible for them—they didn't leave. They had been conditioned to endure the pain. Victims are familiar to losing battles and feeling as if they have no power. They do not believe they can win. Being assertive is a very difficult concept for an incest victim.

The victim's inability to trust affects her feelings about members of the opposite sex. Women who have been abused by men will often not trust them as a whole and believe they only "want one thing". Boys who are abused by more than one male many times believe they must be homosexual.

Many victims of incest confuse sex with affection and love. Since the victim desperately needs validation, this person is likely to become promiscuous. She thinks that if someone has sex with her then he must love her.

MY "Ah ha" Moment: Well, this research really explained a lot. The lack of trust in people, sex as love, making excuses for others, obesity and an eating disorder, living a fantasy family life, promiscuity, etc…. If I had never taken it upon myself to research this area of my brokenness, I would have never known how I was conditioned. And you must know how you have been conditioned (invented) so you will know how to re-condition (re-invent) yourself. I suspect I would have continued to move on to the next lover, start another new diet, go to another depression clinic or perhaps contemplate my own suicide again. I've worked effortlessly on this particular area of my life and have moved from victim to survivor. When a victim grows tired of the consequences and becomes willing to work hard on the incest issue, he or she is on their way to living life as a survivor instead of a victim.

I know you've heard it said "the past is the past, move on". I agree to some point, yet I also believe you must obtain the truths of the past, prepare for proper healing, take the healing journey and *only then* move on...slowly and consistently reinventing your life.

I have made it my life purpose to help others who struggle with brokenness, no matter where the brokenness was derived from. Today, it could simply be caused by societal conditioning. And from the many people who are hurting that I have had the opportunity to meet and to assist with their healing, their conditioning did in fact come from societal conditioning. I have also made a commitment to myself and to God to do all I can do while I am on this earth to educate parents, teachers, counselors and anyone who will listen to me regarding the signs and illnesses associated with childhood sexual abuse and their lifelong effects on the victims. If I am able to save just one little girl or boy from losing her/his life to this devastation, it will have been worth all my heartfelt efforts.

Today, I am an expert in holistic inner child healing, an author, speaker, board member of our local children's advocacy center and a certified Heal Your Life® workshop leader and teacher. I was directly trained by Dr. Patricia Crane, who studied personally with Louise Hay, and partner Rick Nichols, the greatest storyteller on the planet. Heart Inspired Presentations, LLC, is licensed by Hay House, Inc. I was honored to be trained by this amazing woman who has assisted so many people with their own individual healing and presented them with tools to begin their personal journeys toward living the beautiful lives they were created to live. The few of us located around the globe who are certificated and licensed to teach the philosophy of Louise Hay feel it is a privilege to be associated with her in this manner.

I recall vividly back when I was in first grade. Our class was singing a song for a school concert. It was my favorite song, and I found myself singing it through all my years. It went like this, *"Let there be peace on earth, and let it begin with me."*

ABOUT THE AUTHOR
www.lisahardwick.com

Lisa A. Hardwick
is an expert in holistic inner child
healing, a licensed *Heal Your
Life*® teacher, author, speaker,
workshop leader and a board
member for her local chapter
Children's Advocacy Center in
East Central Illinois.

She resides in Charleston, Illinois,
where she enjoys spending time
with her three adult sons, her
parents and an abundance of
friends. She also enjoys traveling
throughout the world, sharing her
testimony and assisting others
on their path to an authentic and
beautiful life.

RESOURCES

The following list of resources are for the national headquarters; search in your yellow pages under "Community Services" for your local resource agencies and support groups.

AIDS

CDC National AIDS Hotline
(800) 342-2437

ALCOHOL ABUSE

Al-Anon Family Group
Headquarters
1600 Corporate Landing Parkway
Virginia Beach, VA 23454-5617
(888) 4AL-ANON
www.al-anon.alateen.org

Alcoholics Anonymous (AA)
General Service Office
475 Riverside Dr., 11th Floor
New York, NY 10115
(212) 870-3400
www.alcoholics-anonymous.org

Children of Alcoholics Foundation
164 W. 74th Street
New York, NY 10023
(800) 359-COAF
www.coaf.org

Mothers Against Drunk Driving
MADD
P.O. Box 541688
Dallas, TX 75354
(800) GET-MADD
www.madd.org

National Association of Children of
Alcoholics (NACoA)
11426 Rockville Pike, #100
Rockville, MD 20852
(888) 554-2627
www.nacoa.net

Women for Sobriety
P.O. Box 618
Quartertown, PA 18951
(215) 536-8026
www.womenforsobriety.org

CHILDREN'S RESOURCES

Child Molestation
Childhelp USA/Child Abuse Hotline
15757 N. 78th St.
Scottsdale, AZ 85260
(800) 422-4453
www.childhelpusa.org

Prevent Child Abuse America
200 South Michigan Avenue, 17th Floor
Chicago, IL 60604
(312) 663-3520
www.preventchildabuse.org

Crisis Intervention
Girls and Boys Town National Hotline
(800) 448-3000
www.boystown.org

Children's Advocacy Center of East Central Illinois
(If your heart feels directed to make a donation to this center, please include Lisa Hardwick's name in the memo – she would be most grateful)
616 6th Street
Charleston, IL 61920
(217) 345-8250
http://caceci.org

Children of the Night
14530 Sylvan St.
Van Nuys, CA 91411
(800) 551-1300
www.childrenofthenight.org

Covenant House Hotline
(800) 999-9999
www.covenanthouse.org

National Children's Advocacy Center
210 Pratt Avenue
Huntsville, AL 35801
(256) 533-KIDS (5437)
www.nationalcac.org

CO-DEPENDENCY

Co-Dependents Anonymous
P.O. Box 33577
Phoenix, AZ 85067
(602) 277-7991
www.codependents.org

SUICIDE, DEATH, GRIEF

AARP Grief and Loss Programs
(800) 424-3410
www.aarp.org/griefandloss

Grief Recovery Institute
P.O. Box 6061-382
Sherman Oaks, CA 91413
(818) 907-9600
www.grief-recovery.com

Suicide Awareness Voices of Education
(SAVE)
Minneapolis, MN 55424
(952) 946-7998

Suicide National Hotline
(800) 784-2433

DOMESTIC VIOLENCE

National Coalition Against Domestic Violence
P.O. Box 18749
Denver, CO 80218
(303) 831-9251
www.ncadv.org

National Domestic Violence Hotline
P.O. Box 161810
Austin, TX 78716
(800) 799-SAFE
www.ndvh.org

DRUG ABUSE

Cocaine Anonymous National Referral Line
(800) 347-8998

National Helpline of Phoenix House
(800) COCAINE
www.drughelp.org

National Institute of Drug Abuse (NIDA)
6001 Executive Blvd., Room 5213, Bethesda, MD 20892-9561, Parklawn Building
Info: (301) 443-6245
Help: (800) 662-4357
www.nida.nih.gov

EATING DISORDER

Overeaters Anonymous
National Office
P.O. Box 44020
Rio Rancho, NM 87174-4020
(505) 891-2664
www.overeatersanonymous.org

GAMBLING

Gamblers Anonymous
International Service Office
P.O. Box 17173
Los Angeles, CA 90017
(213) 386-8789
www.gamblersanonymous.org

HEALTH ISSUES

American Chronic Pain Association
P.O. Box 850
Rocklin, CA 95677
(916) 632-0922
www.theacpa.org

American Holistic Health Association
P.O. Box 17400
Anaheim, CA 92817
(714) 779-6152
www.ahha.org

The Chopra Center at La Costa Resort and Spa
Deepak Chopra, M.D.
2013 Costa Del Mar
Carlsbad, CA 92009
(760) 494-1600
www.chopra.com

The Mind-Body Medical Institute
110 Francis St., Ste. 1A
Boston, MA 02215
(617) 632-9530 Ext. 1
www.mbmi.org

National Health Information Center
P.O. Box 1133
Washington, DC 20013-1133
(800) 336-4797
www.health.gov/NHIC

Preventive Medicine Research Institute
Dean Ornish, M.D.
900 Brideway, Ste 2
Sausalito, CA 94965
(415) 332-2525
www.pmri.org

MENTAL HEALTH

**American Psychiatric Association
of America**
1400 K St. NW
Washington, DC 20005
(888) 357-7924
www.psych.org

**Anxiety Disorders Association of
America**
11900 Parklawn Dr., Ste. 100
Rockville, MD 20852
(310) 231-9350
www.adaa.org

**The Help Center of the American
Psychological Association**
(800) 964-2000
www.helping.apa.org

**National Center for Post Traumatic
Stress Disorder**
(802) 296-5132
www.ncptsd.org

**National Alliance for the
Mentally Ill**
2107 Wilson Blvd., Ste. 300
Arlington, VA 22201
(800) 950-6264
www.nami.org

National Depressive and Manic-
Depressive Association
730 N. Franklin St., Ste. 501
Chicago, IL 60610
(800) 826-3632
www.ndmda.org

National Institute of
Mental Health
6001 Executive Blvd.
Room 81884, MSC 9663
Bethesda, MD 20892
(301) 443-4513
www.nimh.nih.gov

SEX ISSUES

Rape, Abuse and Incest National Network
(800) 656-4673
www.rainn.org

National Council on Sexual Addiction and Compulsivity
P.O. Box 725544
Atlanta, GA 31139
(770) 541-9912
www.ncsac.org

SMOKING

Nicotine Anonymous World Services
419 Main St., PMB #370
Huntington Beach, CA 92648
(415) 750-0328
www.nicotine-anonymous.org

STRESS ISSUES

The Biofeedback & Psychophysiology Clinic
The Menninger Clinic
P.O. Box 829
Topeka, KS 66601-0829
(800) 351-9058
www.menninger.edu

New York Open Center
83 Spring St.
New York, NY 10012
(212) 219-2527
www.opencenter.org

The Stress Reduction Clinic Center for Mindfulness
University of Massachusetts
Medical Center
55 Lake Ave., North
Worcester, MA 01655
(508) 856-2656

TEEN

Al-Anon/Alateen
1600 Corporate Landing
Parkway
Virginia Beach, VA 23454-5617
(888) 425-2666
www.al-anon.alateen.org

Planned Parenthood
810 Seventh Ave.
New York, NY 10019
(800) 230-PLAN
www.plannedparenthood.org

Hotlines for Teenagers
Girls and Boys Town National
Hotline
(800) 448-3000

Childhelp National Child Abuse Hotline
(800) 422-4453

Just for Kids Hotline
(888) 594-KIDS

National Child Abuse Hotline
(800) 792-5200

National Runaway Hotline
(800) 621-4000

National Youth Crisis Hotline
(800)-HIT-HOME

Suicide Prevention Hotline
(800) 827-7571

BIBLIOGRAPHY

Benson, Herbert. (1975).
The Relaxation Response.
New York, NY. Harper Torch

Canfield, Jack (2005).
*The Success Principles: How to Get from
Where You Are to Where You Want to Be.*
New York, NY: Collins

Crane, Patricia. (2002).
*Ordering from the Cosmic Kitchen:
The Essential Guide to Powerful, Nourishing Affirmations.*
Health Horizons

Hay, Louise.(1987).
You Can Heal Your Life.
Carson, CA., Hay

Gilbert, Daniel. (2005).
Stumbling on Happiness.
New York, NY. Vintage

Gilligan, Stephen. (1997).
*The Courage to Love: Principles and
Practices of Self-Relations Psychotherapy.*
New York, NY. W.W. Norton &Company

Goleman, Daniel. (1995).
Emotional Intelligence: Why it can matter more than IQ.
New York, NY: Bantam Dell

BIBLIOGRAPHY *(cont.)*

Landrum, Gene. (2005).
The Superman Syndrome: You Are What You Believe.
Lincoln, NE. iUniverse

Neill, Michael. (2006).
You Can Have What You Want:
Proven Strategies for Inner and Outer Success.
Hayhouse

Tolle, Eckhart. (1999.)
The Power of Now: A Guide to Spiritual Enlightenment.
Novato, CA. New World Library.

Wolinsky, Stephen. (1991).
Trances People Live:
Healing Approaches In Quantum Psychology.
Falls Village, CT. The Bramble Company

Williamson, Marianne. (2009).
The Age of Miracles: Embracing the New Midlife.
Carlsbad, CA. Hay House

INDEX

LaVergne, TN USA
30 January 2011
214544LV00003B/1/P